READING
IS SEEING

**Learning to Visualize Scenes, Characters, Ideas, and
Text Worlds to Improve Comprehension and Reflective Reading**

BY JEFF WILHELM
BOISE STATE UNIVERSITY

NEW YORK • TORONTO • LONDON • AUCKLAND • SYDNEY
MEXICO CITY • NEW DELHI • HONG KONG • BUENOS AIRES

DEDICATION

This effort is dedicated to four special friends and teachers:

Bill Bedford, the Wachsmeister
Paul Corrigan, the Old Animal
Bruce Hunter, the Counselor
Sandip Wilson, the Great-Hearted

You live out loud
and teach by letting your lives speak.
You inspire me and I am grateful.

Cover design by Gerard Fuchs

Interior design by Holly Grundon

Cover photograph by Michael C. York

Interior photographs on pages 18, 21, 29, 45, 98 by Michael C. York

All other interior photographs by Karen Baicker

Page 116,L: American Gothic by Grant Wood. Gift of Friends of the American Art Collection. All rights reserved by the Art Institute of Chicago and VAGA, New York, NY. Image of "American Gothic" supplied by Corbis.

Page 116,R: Gas Mask Gothic by Richard Hess. Used by permission of HessDesignWorks.com.

Page 139, L: Edward Curtis, 1903, from the Collections of the Library of Congress

Page 139,R: Mike Laurance/Scholastic Photo Archive.

Scholastic has made every effort to identify the correct source for work in this book.
Any work not correctly attributed will be attributed in future editions of this book.

ISBN 0-439-30309-5
Copyright © 2004 by Jeffrey D. Wilhelm
All rights reserved. Published by Scholastic Inc.
Printed in the U.S.A.

1 2 3 4 5 6 7 8 9 10   40   11 10 09 08 07 06 05 04

Contents

ACKNOWLEDGMENTS

My life is filled with teachers. Whenever I have cause to reflect about this, such as when I write the acknowledgements for a project such as this book, I'm truly humbled by the recognition of how much I have learned from my students and fellow teachers. Teachers are those who see us through our life challenges. Anne Lamott writes, "We are not here to see through one another, but to see one another through." The following people have done just that for me. It would be impossible for me to thank everyone who deserves it, but I will try to cover a few of those who deserve a most special thanks.

First and foremost, I must thank my editor Wendy Murray for her careful shepherding of this and past projects for Scholastic. I thank also Ray Coutu, Margery Rosnick, and Terry Cooper at Scholastic for their support.

Heartfelt gratitude goes to Sandip Wilson for taking time out of her busy schedule on several occasions to read this manuscript and for giving me many most excellent suggestions. Karl Androes, director of Whirlwind and the new Reading in Motion program in Chicago, also read drafts and made helpful suggestions. I'm also grateful to my friends Mary Massie and Karen Boran from the Chicago Teaching Center, and to the rest of the CTC crew, for their brave forays into arts education. Many of their tips and insights helped to seed and extend the work that is reported here.

My heartfelt appreciation and thanks go to my wife Peggy Jo Wilhelm, teacher extraordinaire and my first reader and editor of every draft, and to Tanya Baker, my closest teaching colleague, for contributions too numerous to mention.

I would not be a teacher, nor a writer, except for the influence of my friend and mentor Michael W. Smith, the esteemed researcher George Hillocks, and my own high-school English teachers Bill Strohm and James Blaser, who made me see that teaching is among the most complex, challenging, fulfilling, and worthwhile of life pursuits.

To my many colleagues and friends, I blow my trumpet and raise my sword in a sincere salute. Thanks go to my new colleagues at Boise State University, who have helped me adjust to a new professional situation, particularly Bruce Ballenger, Jackie O'Connor, Bruce Robbins, and Stan Steiner. My thanks to my colleagues and friends in the Maine Writing Project and the National Writing Project, where so many of the best teaching ideas take shape and are shared. And I am constantly cognizant of the continued collegiality of old mentors and teaching partners, like Brian Ambrosius, Bill Anthony, Jim Artesani, Rosemary Bamford, Erv Barnes, Bill Bedford, Ed Brazee, Paul Corrigan, Mike Ford, Paul Friedemann, Stuart Greene, Leon Holley, Jr., Bruce Hunter, Jan Kristo, Craig Martin, Paula Moore, Bruce Nelson, Bruce Novak, Wayne Otto, John Thorpe, Sandip Wilson, Brian White, and Denny Wolfe. And of course extra thanks to my loving family, particularly my dad, Jack Wilhelm; my wife, Peggy Jo; and the most amazing teachers of my life journey: my daring and sometimes dutiful daughters, warriors of faith, lovers of living life to the fullest, Fiona Luray and Jasmine Marie.

In writing this book, I've gleaned ideas from over 22 years of classroom teaching and professional sharing. I've tried my best to trace the provenance of various notions to particular teachers and students but welcome any emendations for those I may have missed.

Introduction

*I*t was lunchtime. I was sitting at my desk in the empty classroom grading a
last few papers when Curtis walked in. Curtis was a bit of a ragamuffin,
dressed mostly in blaze orange, and sporting a thick mop of curly brown
hair. He was a friendly troublemaker, and struggled with reading and the rest
of school despite possessing some obvious smarts. I liked him a lot.

"Curtis!" I called. "What's up?"

He meandered across the room and deposited himself heavily on the couch
next to my desk.

"Ya know, Mr. Wilhelm," he offered. "School just isn't about the kids
anymore."

"How's that?" I asked.

"Teachers just give you a bunch of stuff to do and never help you. And they
don't care what you can do or what you are interested in. They don't pay any
attention to the kids: they just give out the work. Why is it that someone who
doesn't even know us says what kids are supposed to do?"

I wasn't sure what brought on this philosophical lament, and Curtis wasn't
offering any specifics. So to change the subject, and maybe even find out more by
changing the mood, I picked up a poetry book by my friend Paul Corrigan.

"Curtis, I know you like hunting. So I'd like your opinion of this poem. Come
on over beside me so we can read it together."

I read the poem "First Deer" aloud, about Paul's first hunting trip with his
father.

"See!" Curtis said excitedly when I'd finished. "That's just what I mean! That
dad in the poem helped his son see what to do, and then he helped him do it so he
could see and feel and know how to do it on his own. They worked together! That's
how my pops taught me to hunt, too. But they don't do that for you in school."

Show me how. This is what Curtis wanted from me. I couldn't help but feel that he had come to me to ask for help with his reading. And the trust he placed in me made me feel an awesome responsibility.

One of the ways I was able to help Curtis was through the use of visualization strategies, which show kids how to become better readers by making the elements and strategies of the reading process visible and concrete. And in the same way that the father in Corrigan's poem shows his son how to gut a deer by first literally guiding his son's hands, I have tried to teach Curtis and other students over the years in a manner that keeps in sight a novice's need to be supported before working on his or her own.

This book will tell two stories. The first is of how I came to use this process of showing/helping/letting go as I developed and adapted visual strategies to assist my students in their reading. These techniques have been particularly effective for helping my struggling readers, but as I will show, they have powerful effects for all readers, including very accomplished ones.

The second story, which runs like an undercurrent through this book, is of my journey to become a better teacher. This story is about my realization that whenever I did improve my practice, it was because of a challenge thrown out to me by my students; by a failure of my teaching; or by a set of problems I wasn't solving.

There have been many times in my career when I have dismissed these challenges, chalking them up to a student's having a bad day or as some issue beyond my ability to address. But sometimes I have listened hard to my students and scrutinized their actions, knowing that all behavior has meaning. I have tried to learn from them how I could teach them more effectively in order to get them out of whatever box they were in. On these occasions, I've taken risks, tried new ideas, and always learned something that has improved my teaching—even in cases where the innovation failed. And through these experiences, I've earned the right to say to you now: Don't shy away from new ideas. Why? It's better to reflect on why a new idea didn't work out than to do the same old thing. The same old thing won't lead to growth or change for you or your students. You'll just get the same results, and if you have a student like Curtis, that won't cut it.

Curtis was telling me that the way school did things, and the way I was teaching reading, wasn't working for him. That meant that something new must be tried. Thinking back on Curtis now, what comes to mind is that old joke about the teacher who really didn't have 25 years of experience, he just had one year of experience 25 times. I wince a bit every time I remember this joke because despite my success with Curtis, there have been times when inertia kept me from the kind of adventurous teaching that would benefit my students.

In my own journey, I saw that the way to informed change is reflective teaching, a model that undergirds every strategy I discuss in this book. Reflective teaching is a way of cultivating a receptiveness to learning—in yourself and in your students. Reflective teaching is relational. It is a way of paying attention to students so that you can match them with the right texts, techniques, and assistance to help them grow and become strong.

My friend Sheridan Blau, former president of NCTE, says that the beginning teacher focuses on his own teaching; the competent teacher focuses on the connections between teaching and learning and makes use of the professional knowledge base; and the advanced teacher is reflective and analytical, inquiring into teaching by deeply considering student learning and helping students to make connections. This continuum moves from isolation to collaboration, from teaching lessons to a coherent program of teaching relationally over time.

Arthur Applebee calls this kind of teaching "principled practice," a level of teaching that is forever in pursuit of the *why* of teaching: what purposes and ends we are working toward, why we make certain instructional moves, why certain methods work in particular situations with particular kids. Pursuing these questions allow us to use the teaching strategies at our disposal, including the ones described here, in wide-awake and strategic ways.

Frances Schoonmaker says: "To prepare children for a hopeful future, teachers must be able to do more than implement a handful of strategies they have learned in a teacher education program or on the job. They must have an experimental mindset."

Keep these quotes from our esteemed colleagues in mind as you read on and try the visualization strategies I present in this book; they are the philosophical backdrop of these strategies, and they are the heart and soul of what I believe about teaching and learning. I know these visualization strategies will help you assist your students in becoming better readers, and I hope all the background stories will assist you in responding to your students as a reflective practitioner. And with that, let the grand rumpus of experiments begin!

CHAPTER 1

Reading *Is Seeing*

Why Teaching Students to Visualize Is So Important

Close your eyes. Think of a favorite novel— perhaps one from your youth or a current favorite. Recover a favorite scene. For example, I can picture a Hardy Boys mystery: Frank, Joe, and their pudgy friend Chet, who's wearing a red flannel shirt and jeans, bushwhacking

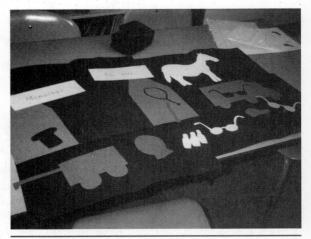

Key images from a book can be emblazoned in our memories for a lifetime. Shown here, a character symbol map expresses the images that are important to the reader.

through the woods in the moonlight. Chet is sweating and breathing hard and muttering "Gee whiz!" whenever a branch slaps him in the face. I next see them untethering a boat and motoring slowly across the wind-whipped ocean waves out to the old lighthouse, dark clouds scudding across the moon.

Interestingly, many of my visual memories are of moving images. But not all. One of the scenes that often came to mind after reading *Independence Day* by Richard Ford was a still-shot of the divorced father sitting alone on the lawn with his young daughter. His daughter is barefoot. My visualization somehow captures for me how alone they were together, yet how intensely they were together in their loneliness. It's a poignant postcard that I carry around in my head that summarizes something important to me about relationships and divorce.

Scenes from our reading can be emblazoned in our memories for a lifetime. These images are a significant part of what makes reading intense, engaging, enjoyable, accessible, and usable—both at the moment of reading and afterwards. Images and the ideas connected to them become a part of us, and we call them forth as tools to help us think about issues or events in our current lives.

Based on my research on engaged reading, I've argued that being able to create images, story worlds, and mental models while one reads is an essential element of reading comprehension, engagement, and reflection (Wilhelm, 1997). In fact, without visualization, students cannot comprehend, and reading cannot be said to be reading.

Our Images
Powerful Elixirs of Text and Self

Now think of a time, maybe when you were a kid, when you saw the movie version of a favorite book and were shocked, perhaps even offended, because the actors didn't look as you had imagined. Or perhaps the scenery and action did not play out in the way they did in your mind while reading. I remember seeing *Fantastic Voyage* as a seventh grader after loving the book. "Who are these impostors?" I recall thinking. "What numskull made this movie?"

The power of the visual experiences we bring to a text, and subsequently create in concert with the text as we read, is intense. What we see is guided by an author's descriptions, but it is an elixir of these cues and our own experiences—

we are the artist, after all, creating each frame of the movie based on the script from the text. Imagining a character might involve conjuring a favorite actor's face, or a combination of a brother's face with a school chum's physiognomy, since reading is a personal transaction with the codes of a text (Rosenblatt, 1978; Wilhelm, 1997).

PICTURING NONFICTION TEXTS

Good readers intensely visualize even when reading nonfiction or informational text. I recently read David McCullough's *John Adams*, and when I think of it, the image that pops into my head is of Adams sitting at a desk late at night, writing a letter to his wife and soulmate Abigail. I imagine candlelight, his books strewn across his writing table, a careworn look on his face as he describes the weighty conflicts and political turmoils he faces without her there to support him.

Even nonfiction books that deliver many facts are often represented in our memories by visuals that typify the character of a person behind the facts or a person who might use the information. For example, to recall your reading of a recipe, you might visualize gathering the necessary ingredients on your counter, pulling out the mixing bowl, and mixing the ingredients.

Good readers also often create visual devices and mental models to organize and store the facts themselves. Even texts that don't offer character or context can be brought to life by doing this. For example, I recently read a magazine article about how making economic predictions assures that the predictions will not come true because the prediction itself changes behavior. While reading the article, I created bar graphs in my mind with blue lines for predictions of surpluses and red ones for actual surpluses. I also imagined a kind of political cartoon of a pile of cash—the predicted surpluses—and ghostly figures representing the future, who were spending it before it could accrue. These visualizations helped me to establish the meaning of what I was reading and put it in a form that summarized that meaning, so that I could interpret and use it.

Whether we're reading fiction or nonfiction, visualizing is central to reading and to thinking with what we read. So how do we harness this power of visualization in our classrooms? How can we use visual strategies to help our struggling readers to do what expert readers do? How can we use the same techniques to extend the abilities of even our better readers to read more challenging texts with greater facility? These are the visualization projects I will explore in this book.

What Are Visualization Strategies?
A Quick Sketch of Them in Action

In later chapters I'll share various strategies and projects in detail, but so you have a good picture of them right away, here's a glimpse of how a bunch of boys I taught in Wisconsin used visualization strategies. I'll spotlight a boy named Scott, who probably had the most to gain from the strategies.

Scott was a student who had been mainstreamed into my EEN (exceptional educational needs) seventh-grade reading/language arts. He was labeled LD and ED and had failed reading the year before, and his sixth-grade teacher had told me that he didn't think Scott could really read. It was clear that Scott was a poor reader who had had several special education labels attached to him during his school history. And he was dragging those labels around, clunking them against each other and himself, like they were the chain carried by Marlow's ghost.

Through informal chats with Scott, I found that he had many interests and that he passionately wanted to be a better reader (mostly so he could read to pursue his interests). He was very frustrated with school, which caused him to act out often; he would sometimes lie on the classroom floor in a near catatonic state of frustration. He said, "School makes me look stupid. Isn't school supposed to make you smart? . . . Nobody helps me to read. Teachers just tell me I'm a bad reader and that I'm always wrong, but nobody helps me." Scott's poor reading clearly caused him many social frustrations as well as academic ones.

When I asked him what he saw when he read, he griped, "I can't see anything. I don't see anything when I read."

I made a deal with Scott. We'd spend lunch periods reading comic books, graphic novels, and picture books on topics related to our classroom work, an idea inspired by Margaret Meek's work with illiterate boys (Meek, et al., 1983). We'd try some visual techniques to help his comprehension. In return, he would try his best and also try to keep his nose clean and out of trouble—as much as was humanly possible!

It was a challenge, but Scott and I both stuck with it. There were some rough patches, but Scott began to slowly, ever so slowly, grow as a reader and become a part of our classroom learning projects.

Later in the school year, I walked into my classroom to find my seventh-grade class abuzz. It was the end of our civil rights unit. We'd been pursuing the question: "What are civil rights, and how can we protect them?" We'd done some reading and activities in common, but now students had teamed up to pursue their own research. Groups of four or five students were working in tight clusters of desks creating picture maps of the major ideas they'd learned so far about their various inquiry questions. Scott was working with a group of five boys, who were sprawled on beanbag chairs.

Two were kids I considered good readers, two were fairly average, and one was Scott. United by their love of baseball, they were inquiring into the experience of black baseball players who played in the Negro Leagues and then helped to break the color line in the major leagues. They wanted to know what it took to successfully break this barrier. They had been focusing on the personal character of players like Jackie Robinson, but their reading had now prompted them to consider other factors as well.

Scott was presenting five big pictures he had created on sheets of chart paper. These were main-idea tableaux, and they visually summarized what he considered to be the main ideas of *Teammates*, a picture book by Peter Goldenbock about the friendship between Brooklyn Dodgers players Pee

A picture map of *Roll of Thunder, Hear My Cry*. A student's complex thinking about relationships in the story is distilled into a few words and pictures.

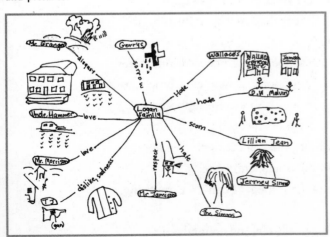

READING IS SEEING

Wee Reese and Jackie Robinson. Under my guidance, Scott had been reading a lot of picture books and easy readers that were appropriate to his ability, and he was learning a lot about his group's topic. He was also making valuable contributions to the group's project, which was to create a video documentary addressing their question. I couldn't help but notice that Scott looked happy, engaged, and involved with his classmates, and that they in turn were listening closely to him and taking him seriously.

Five of Scott's six pictures depicted Jackie Robinson with supportive characters from his life: Negro League players, fans, Branch Rickey (the general manager who invited Jackie to join the Brooklyn Dodgers), and Pee Wee Reese (the white all-star player who did so much to help Jackie overcome the prejudice he faced). Only one of the pictures showed the fans and teammates who resisted Jackie's place on the Dodgers' baseball team. This surprised Scott: "When I was drawing main ideas, I was surprised that most of them were helping instead of hurting pictures. That made me really think."

Scott told his group, "Drawing these made me see how important other people were [to Jackie's successfully breaking the color barrier]. We're right that Jackie put up with lots of prejudice and had to be brave, play good, and not fight back and all that, but he also needed these other people, or he wouldn't have been able to do it. I think we have to include this as part of our answer."

As Scott talked, Robin was busily adding the categories "black leaders," "black teammates," "fans," "white leaders," and "white teammates" to the semantic-feature analysis the group had been making to keep track of what helped or hindered various players, such as Jackie Robinson and Hank Aaron, in their efforts to be successful in the major leagues.

Steven jotted notes. "We definitely have to show two of Scott's scenes in our video," he chimed. "The one with Branch Rickey and

> ## "All thought depends upon the image."
>
> *Ferdinand de Saussure,*
> *the father of modern semiotics*

CONSIDER THIS

In inquiry frameworks for curriculum, every student can progress from their own current abilities and interests, do different kinds of work, and still contribute to the common learning project of the classroom. Since students negotiate their own research questions and readings around the central topic, teaching can be naturally differentiated, and individual needs accommodated.

the one where Pee Wee puts his arm around Jackie in Cincinnati. " As the other boys nodded, he started to sketch out a storyboard that would fit these scenes into their developing documentary.

Throughout their project, the boys used visualization strategies for various purposes:

- Scott used the tableaux (something we had worked on during our lunches together) to help himself comprehend his reading: to visualize scenes, identify main ideas, generate new ideas, and placehold these for sharing with his group members.

- Robin contributed to the group's semantic-feature analysis, a guide to seeing patterns across the various texts group members had read.

- Steven sketched a storyboard that provided a format for sequencing and representing various ideas for their video documentary, a visual project that engaged the boys and focused their discussion and learning.

Throughout, the visuals helped the boys to read, respond, analyze, organize, and represent their learning. These tools leveled the playing field, allowing weaker readers to elbow into the contest by making accessible the strategies of expert players of the reading game, and by extending the abilities of the accomplished readers.

The Benefits
of Visualization Strategies

A wide research base indicates that visualization strategies can:

- heighten motivation, engagement, and enjoyment of reading, particularly for struggling readers;

- increase time spent on reading tasks;

- improve literal comprehension of both narrative and expository text;

- improve integration of what is learned with existing background knowledge (schematics);

- build schematic background knowledge around topics; images serve as "mental pegs" on which further info can be hooked and built;

- provide a template that supports the use of more sophisticated comprehension strategies, such as inferring, elaborating, and discerning main ideas and themes;

- act as a "lever tool" —a central technique that gives readers access to many other skills and forms of response;

- increase the ability to elaborate on characters, scenes, actions, ideas;

- aid in identifying important details and knitting them together to make inferences, see patterns of a text's ideas and organization;

- improve the ability to see connections: to compare the ideas of two or more texts, see the patterns of ideas expressed across multiple texts, and to link ideas to the world;

- develop awareness of one's reading processes (metacognition);

- increase aesthetic appreciation of text;

- improve a reader's ability to share, critique, and revise what has been learned with others;

- help in solving spatial and verbal problems; e.g., story problem in math, process descriptions;

- hone composing skills in various forms, including writing, helping readers become aware of composing techniques and their effects;

- aid general problem solving;

- improve test scores on various reading measures, including standardized tests.

(See Gambrell and Koskinen 2001; Wilhelm, 1995, 1997 for research reviews)

Two Key Research-Proven Highlights

Visualization improves key comprehension skills: Imagery and visualization treatments have achieved demonstrable success in various kinds of studies of the most intractable instructional problems around improving reading. For example, visualization has been successful in improving comprehension monitoring, a skill integral to expert reading, identifying main ideas and justifying these with evidence from a text, and seeing patterns of details across a text or texts to discover complex implied relationships (an essential tool for thinking and learning). These are skills that, according to recent National Assessments of Educational Progress, fewer than six percent of our high school seniors can effectively use. (See e.g. Jerry and Lutkus, NAEP, 2003)

Visualization improves test scores in reading: Even cursory use of instruction supporting visualization improves scores on standardized tests. Personally, I do not hold stock in standardized test scores. I am convinced that such tests miss what is most important about reading and writing achievement and at the same time serve to dumb down both teaching and learning (see *The Testing Trap* Hillocks, 2001, for a powerful study demonstrating how this is so). Nonetheless, I work in schools and know the political realities of test scores. Some ingenious studies (see especially Rose, et al, 2000, and the Arts Education Partnerships Critical Links study, 2002, www.aep-arts.org) have shown that imagery use has many benefits, including higher standardized reading scores relative to control groups.

THE SOCIAL ADVANTAGE

In addition to the research-based benefits of visualization strategies, there are some other documented and common sense ones I'd like to highlight. First, students read visual texts in many arenas: cartoons, television shows and movies, websites, other multimedia texts, and so on. So it makes sense to use visuals in the classroom to link school reading with these other cultural literacies. Indeed, we must value and use these cultural resources—and kids' facility with them—to reach and teach them as readers and writers. Let them engage this "outside" expertise to strengthen areas of their literacy that can be improved.

Second, inviting children to create visual responses to texts is an effective bridge to other composing literacies, such as writing and multimedia design.

Third, by embracing a wide variety of literacies in the classroom, you invite opportunities for students to interact and collaborate together that often don't occur in traditional reading and writing instructional settings. Let's face it, we all like company, and students in upper elementary and middle school may be at the height of this need to socialize. Visualization projects are wonderfully interactive.

And last, when students compose and explore ideas together through various literacies, such as murals, newspapers, websites, and videos, they gain access to democratic avenues of meaning making. After all,

A student expresses her understanding of the changing states of matter through a cartoon. As teachers, we need to involve kids in many types of literate expression.

"communities of practice" in the real world use multiple literacies to solve problems and negotiate meanings—why shouldn't our students? In offering them many viable literacies, we apprentice them for real-world activities, where they will be required to demonstrate their understanding in many ways, including making visual products.

Despite these many research-proven benefits for both struggling and accomplished readers, a review of instructional materials and textbooks reveals that visual strategies are rarely presented or encouraged. This leaves it to us, the teachers, to provide students with visual strategies that are appropriate to their needs as readers.

CHAPTER 2

What Does It Mean to Teach?

Grounding our Instruction in Current Research and Theory

W hen Curtis stopped by to see me that lunchtime and lamented that school "isn't about the kids any more," I read him a poem to lift his spirits, a poem about a subject I knew he knew well: hunting. That this poem about a father teaching his son would move him to say, "People in real life teach each other that way, but teachers never do" and thereby lay out a challenge for all teachers in our school—well, that I didn't predict. But I was glad because it gave me a window into his need.

Everything we do as teachers expresses a theory about reading, about learning, and about what we think is important.

Curtis went on to tell me that he was having trouble in math because he couldn't understand word problems. I said I would try to help him. Now, I had several choices. I could have lectured Curtis on the mathematical principles he needed. I could have shown him correctly solved word problems, hoping he'd be able to tease out the thinking processes involved, but that seemed a bit like trying to teach someone to play the saxophone by having them listen to John Coltrane CDs. Or I could have just urged Curtis to keep fiddling around with the assigned word problems until he "discovered" how to do them.

I chose another course, albeit a rare one in American schools. We went through the math book and found some word problems about maple sugaring, since he had done some sugaring on his uncle's farm. I then "thought aloud" about how I would do one of these problems in three steps. I drew pictures of the process and created a chart that showed the available data and the data that was missing. After my think-aloud, Curtis and I identified all the strategies I used. We discussed other ways of solving the problem and the advantages and pitfalls of each. Then I did another problem and asked Curtis to help me at various points. After a few more problems, Curtis took the lead and I helped him (if other students had been around, I would have had them help each other), and by the end of the period Curtis completed a word problem on his own.

Curtis departed a few minutes before the bell, saying, "I think I've kind of got it now." Off he went, exiting my room and heading out into the stream of humanity heading up from the lunchroom. Spinning a paper clip in my hand, I thought about Curtis, who would be out on his own in the world one day. I hoped I had used a process of assistance that would let him do some of the work of mathematicians wherever in life this kind of thinking would be required of him.

In the past I might have just told Curtis what to do or to figure it out on his own. But studying, reflecting on my own learning, and considering how various methods of teaching helped struggling readers led me to the learning-centered style of teaching I used with Curtis. This didn't happen overnight. My journey to learning-centered teaching was filled with frustrations and missteps.

Teaching as a Theoretical Battleground

Now I'll lay my cards on the table: in this chapter I'm going to try to lead you to see why learning-centered teaching is the superior stance. Even if I don't convince you, you'll walk away at chapter's end with the research-based theoretical backdrop for the teaching ideas in this book. I will put in boldface the points I'd like you to carry away and "tattoo on your forehead," (as I put it to the pre-service teachers I coach).

ALL TEACHING IS THEORETICAL.

Many teachers I've talked with profess to have little patience with theory. They argue that they are on the front lines, dealing with individual students' needs each day, so they don't have time for "pie in the sky" stuff. In fact, every dealing we undertake and every decision we make is theoretical. We do what we do and decide what we decide because of beliefs that this teaching "move" will work in this situation with this child or this group. Being unaware of our theories means we cannot test them—consider how happy we are with them—which keeps us from improving them in ways that would benefit our own teaching and our students' learning. This keeps us from achieving the reflective practice of a professional teacher.

EVERYTHING WE DO IN A CLASSROOM EXPRESSES A THEORY OF LEARNING.

When I walk into a classroom and see a lectern in the front and all the desks in rows, I see a theory expressed. What is revealed is a teacher-centered content-oriented view that the teacher has the information students need and will purvey it to them through talk. If the classroom has learning centers and small clusters of desks, an entirely different theory is expressed: a student-centered or learning-centered outlook that believes students will learn best by engaging in projects that they work on together, with the help of the teacher.

UNDERSTANDING THEORY MAKES OUR TEACHING MORE POWERFUL.

Understanding the theoretical foundations of the ideas in this book will help you use teaching and reading strategies to much greater effect. Instead of getting a grab bag of ideas, I want you to have a powerful lens for thinking about teaching and learning—and teaching and learning reading in particular. Understanding the theoretical underpinnings will allow you to adapt all of the ideas here, and to invent new ones, depending on the needs and situations of your students.

THERE ARE THREE MAJOR THEORIES IN AMERICAN EDUCATION THAT CONTEND WITH EACH OTHER.

All debates and disagreements in education boil down to three conflicting theories about teaching and learning. Debates about accountability (how do

Every teacher must ask and answer theoretical questions like "How can I best teach *my* students to read?"

we know that students have learned?), about standardized testing (what measures prove learning?), about whole language versus phonics (is meaning in the text, in the reader's head, or somewhere in between?) and about curricular content and emphases (what texts should we teach in sixth grade versus seventh grade?) are all theoretical in nature. Sides are chosen based on beliefs about effective teaching and learning.

In the first chapters of *Strategic Reading* (2001), my co-authors and I offer a thorough review of these three theories and how they are paralleled by theories of reading and literary interpretation. We explore the affects of these theories on teaching practices and student performance. I give only an overview of the theories here and refer those interested to *Strategic Reading* and the cited research into human cognition.

The Curriculum-Centered Model

Barbara Rogoff (Rogoff, et al, 1996), the famous cognitive scientist, classifies the first theoretical family as "curriculum-centered," though it is also known as teacher-centered, information-centered, or content-centered. Interestingly, curriculum is a Latin word meaning "the racecourse." In this theory, the racecourse is laid out and students are made to run it exactly as it is laid out. The central idea is that teachers possess the information that students need, and students can receive this from the teacher. This theory dominates American schools and the teaching of reading.

Curriculum-Centered: Some Key Ideas

◆ Orientation is bottom up—students learn the parts, then put them together into a whole.

◆ Behaviorism and information-processing theories support this model.

◆ Focus is on the WHAT—the information to be learned, the behavior to be adopted.

◆ Teaching is transmission through the purveying of information—lectures, reading assignments, drills and worksheets, rewards and punishments.

◆ Learning is receiving information—listening, taking notes, reading.

◆ Learning is assessed by tests or discussions that require recapitulation of information.

A student reads poetry. Does a poem's meaning reside entirely in the text? People who support a curriculum-centered approach would probably say yes.

- Reading is the decoding of textual information.

- Reading is based on the decoding of phonemes.

- Meaning is in the text.

- Comprehension is the ability to recapitulate the presented material.

- New Criticism/traditional literary theories are consistent with this model.

- Valid interpretation requires identifying what the text expresses.

- To teach reading, teach kids phonics and reading strategies separately from reading, and then they will then be able to apply it to their reading.

- Understanding the content of important texts makes us better readers.

The Student-Centered Model

A progressive alternative to curriculum-centered approaches is called the "student-centered" model (Rogoff, et al.) This approach is also variously called natural learning, discovery learning, or constructivism. The basic tenet is that students are not empty vessels to be filled up like Ragu jars with the spaghetti sauce of knowledge; they are active meaning-makers who must construct their own understandings. These cannot be provided pre-packaged by a teacher. An apt metaphor for learning in this model would be the "individual path." The idea is that students are naturally programmed to learn and will learn from their experiences, if we create stimulating environments for them. They cannot learn by following a pre-ordained racecourse and they cannot be written on like blank slates; they must walk their own path and construct their own understandings.

Student-Centered: Some Key Ideas

- Orientation is top down—all learning begins with student interests and the big picture.

- Theories of cognitivism, progressivism, and constructivism support this model.

- Focus is on the WHO, the LEARNER—the students' interests and needs of the moment.

- Teaching is creating an environment in which kids can naturally develop, allowing them to self-select readings and projects

- Learning is constructing one's own understandings—it is a *natural* result of human development as learners

interact with
various materials.
Learning proceeds in
set stages determined
by psychosocial
development.

With the student-centered approach, the child's interests drive the curriculum.

◆ Reading is
constructing
personally meaningful responses to the world's various
"texts"—representions of meaning.

◆ Reading requires using one's life experiences to
make meaning.

◆ Meaning is in the reader.

◆ Comprehension is the ability to construct a meaningful
personal response.

◆ Subjective Reader Response literary
theories are consistent with this model.

◆ Valid interpretation accounts for the reader's needs.

◆ To teach reading, provide lots of materials and choice;
allow kids to pursue their own reading agendas and
interests, so they can develop naturally. Reading a lot
makes us better readers.

The Learning-Centered Model

Rogoff proposes that research in cognitive science over the past 30 years demonstrates that we need a "two-sided" model. This model focuses on the relationship between the teacher and learner, the text and the reader, and on the relationship between the knowledge (emphasizing strategic processes to be learned) and the contexts, or "community of practice," in which such knowledge is learned and will be used. She calls this approach the "learning-centered" model, though it is alternatively known as sociocultural, Vygotskian, teaching/learning-centered, and co-constructivist. The purpose of this model is to "transform the participation" of learners from that of novices into that of expert practitioners who are actually involved in whatever field of endeavor is associated with the knowledge domain under study.

Interestingly, Miles Myers, the former executive director of the National Council of Teachers of English (NCTE), argues forcefully in his book *Changing Our Minds* (1996) that the literacy taught in school is always 30 years or more behind the literacy demands and uses of current society. This is because teaching is typically seen as donating established sets of information instead of as apprenticing students to "communities of practice" that actually use literate practices to do things in the real world. Likewise, the cognitive researcher Rich Lehrer from the University of Wisconsin makes the point, in a personal communication, that teaching in schools is almost always 30 to 50 years behind the research understandings in cognition and learning.

With the learning-centered approach the interactions between teachers and students in the context of meaningful situations are crucial.

Learning-Centered: Some Key Ideas

◆ Orientation is interactive/transactional—learning must attend to student interests and goals AND the cultural knowledge to be learned from using the text.

◆ Theories of socioculturalism and co-constructivism support this model.

◆ Focus is on the HOW—the CONTEXT and RELATIONSHIPS in which the procedures of knowledge production and performance are learned.

◆ Teaching is assisting learners to do what they cannot yet do on their own, in the context of real situations in which the learning is necessary and useful.

◆ Learning is not natural but *cultural*—knowledge is socially and culturally constructed, so learning is a result of the opportunities and assistance provided by more knowledge-able practitioners of the studied material and processes.

◆ Reading is constructing understanding through conversing and transacting with a text, attending to the cultural codes it expresses and the way it has been constructed.

◆ Reading requires using one's life experiences and attending to the cultural conventions and meanings that a text uses to communicate.

◆ Meaning is in the conversation between the reader and the text, where the reader's needs and interests meet the communicated meanings of the text.

◆ Comprehension is the ability to construct a meaningful personal response that is respectful of and attends to the text's communicated meaning.

◆ Authorial and Transactional Reader-Response theories of literary experience and interpretation are consistent with this model.

◆ Valid interpretation accounts for the reader's needs *and* the coded meanings of the text.

◆ To teach reading, provide assistance to students who are reading challenging texts to undertake real-world projects or address real-world issues. Becoming a better reader requires help using new strategies and understanding sophisticated textual conventions in meaningful contexts—analogous to those in which literacy is used in the real world.

THE THEORIES AT WORK IN THIS BOOK

I wholeheartedly throw my lot in with the learning-centered folks, based on my own learning, teaching experiences, research with student readers, reading of the current research bases in cognition and reading, and reading of the Russian psychologist Lev Vygotsky and his followers.

I am a learning-centered teacher. The apprenticeship model makes the most sense to me as a parent, a teacher, and researcher.

To be fair, all three theories "work," but to different ends. Curriculum-centered approaches work to temporarily change student behavior or to temporarily learn material for a test (a long tradition of research shows that 80% of the material memorized for such purposes is quickly forgotten; cf., Tyler, 1949). Student-centered approaches can be very successful at helping kids to engage and to improve at what they already have some facility in doing. Anyone endorsing these "one-sided" approaches can garner evidence that their approach works. The essential question is what end is achieved by each, and how these ends match the benefits we want our students to attain. I personally want my students to develop new interests based on their old ones, to develop new abilities, and to continually outgrow themselves. I want them to be more powerful learners and citizens both today (immediately) and tomorrow (in the future) by understanding and participating in various communities of practice in ways that at least simulate those of experts.

I cannot possibly convey how passionately I believe in this approach. My professional life is inhabited by students who suffer intensely in school, never seeing the payoff of true learning. Like Curtis, many poignantly understand that school fails to meet their human needs, and fails utterly to teach them. The fact that there is a powerful alternative endorsed by more than 30 years of research in literacy and cognitive science that is rarely used drives me to distraction. It's as if doctors were still bleeding patients and using leeches long after it had been established that such a practice was not only unhelpful but deleterious.

The Learning-Centered Model
Important Tenets

Below are a few of the important features of the learning-centered model.

ALL LEARNING IS SOCIAL AND TRANSACTIONAL.

A student, or indeed any learner, learns by transacting with another consciousness (through direct interaction or through a text, such as a book or website).

Bruner (1986), using Vygotsky, argues that the driving force behind all learning is social interaction in the context of "joint productive activity" (completing a significant task with the help of others more expert) as opposed to being told something (curriculum-centered) or being encouraged to do something on one's own (student-centered).

LEARNING IS AN APPRENTICESHIP TO A COMMUNITY OF PRACTICE.

Learning transactions are an entry into particular cultures or communities of practice that make, use, and perform knowledge. This might mean entry into a content domain, such as science, a trade, such as carpentry, or a group of readers, such as science-fiction or fantasy aficionados. To be inducted into the culture, you must be taught the language, strategies, goals, and other cultural knowledge by more expert practitioners in that culture because the knowledge does not exist apart from it. For example, you are in a restaurant and order a bacon, lettuce and tomato sandwich on lightly toasted rye bread and a Beefeater Martini straight up with a twist. The waiter writes Bf (M)/↑(tw), slaps the slip on the cocktail counter, and then yells through the grill window: "BLT on whiskey down!" Learning to be a waiter means learning certain procedures, terms, and codes. Listen to bridge players or golfers discuss their games, and it will be just as rich. In short, these groups use lingo with a lot of specialized knowledge behind it.

KNOWING HOW TO DO SOMETHING MEANS BEING FLUENT IN THE LANGUAGE AND STRATEGIES OF THAT PERFORMANCE.

When I learned to whitewater kayak, I had to learn not only the skills of eskimo rolling, "peeling out" into heavy current, and "eddying in" to calm water but also this vocabulary and how to use it to "see" the river—plan and execute "catches" of "micro-eddies" (small quiet pools of water in whitewater from which one can "scout" or rest), plan "lines" (routes) through rocky descents, and use "sweeps," "boofs," and other moves to execute these "lines." Learning these strategies and terms was part of the entry into the cultural knowledge of the kayaking fraternity; it was how I became a full-fledged member of this "culture" or community of practice.

WHAT IS LEARNED MUST BE TAUGHT.

A tenet of Vygotskian theory is that what is learned must be taught, precisely because it is cultural and conventional—it is not natural, like, say, learning to walk. Particular groups of people have created the knowledge, invented the terminology, and devised the appropriate procedures as they practiced certain kinds of activities together. To join, you must be taught their forms of special knowledge. Visual tools are an excellent way of doing this, since they make sophisticated, abstract strategies and content visible and available to learners.

LEARNERS MOVE ON A CONTINUUM FROM NOVICE PRACTICE TO MORE EXPERT PRACTICE.

So how do we give children the lingo and moves they need to get into the expert reading club? This is where Vygotsky's concept of the "zone of proximal development" (ZPD) is useful. Vygotsky defines the ZPD as "the distance between the actual developmental level (of the learner) as determined by independent problem-solving and the level of potential development as determined through problem-solving under adult guidance or in collaboration with more capable peers." In other words, what students can already do, we should allow them to do on their own. (This is a student's "independent learning" level.) What they cannot do on their own but can do with our help (called the "instructional level") should be the substance of what we teach them.

Teaching is providing assistance to the child to do what she cannot yet do on her own.

The assistance we provide students with to be successful in meeting new challenges (which they could not meet on their own) is the stuff of teaching. In this book visualization strategies comprise the powerful teaching support that assists students through their ZPD.

Good teaching is always in the learner's zone of proximal development.

Students asked to work only at their independent level do what they can already do and learn nothing new. What students cannot do successfully even with assistance is something they should not be asked to do (such tasks are at their "frustrational level"). Students who cannot be successful with a task even if we help them end up learning worse than nothing—they learn that reading is too hard or stupid or that they are not readers. Useful teaching proceeds in the ZPD, the student's instructional learning level.

Different students have different ZPDs, so instructional methods must be flexible.

A significant challenge to teachers is that all students in a classroom have somewhat different zones of proximal development. This means that we have to recognize their different zones and teach them in ways that assist them through those zones to higher levels of actual development. Visualization strategies are great for this because they are so flexible. They can be used to help both struggling readers and more advanced readers to improve from their own level and become more competent readers using particular strategies, such as reading for main ideas. Visual techniques are ways to meet all learners in their ZPD and assist them at their current level of reading accomplishment. Likewise, learning-centered inquiry environments allow students to read different texts that are appropriate for them and to be taught in slightly different ways, while still engaging in a common classroom project.

BUILDING FROM THE KNOWN TO THE NEW

Okay, so teaching and learning are social and relational, what we learn is cultural and is used to solve problems, and the ZPD is the window for new learning. There is one more central sociocultural insight for you to put in your pocket: *To learn something new we have to use our current resources and connect what is already known to the new.*

In cognitive research, this has long been known as a basic tenet of schema theory. A schema is an organized set of all information you know about a particular topic or

We bring all we've experienced in life to each and every text we read.

issue. This knowledge is systematic and patterned and usually includes a repertoire of strategies to help solve problems. Learning requires that existing schema be used and then either added to (accommodated) or revised and restructured (adapted) in the face of the new learning.

When expert readers read, they immediately access schematic knowledge to visualize and build meaning. What background do you access when you read the following statement? What do you think it is about?

Blinds for sale

This statement usually causes readers to begin imagining venetian blinds and

THE ZPD

Students all possess a current zone of actual development—their current independent abilities.

The ZPD defines the lower and upper limits of successful instruction. If teaching is pitched too high and students cannot be successful even with help, then students will become frustrated and not learn. If it is too low, then students simply repeat what they already know.

The ZPD for any student is not a "fixed attribute" but is co-constructed through teacher-student relationships around particular tasks (Gordon Wells, 1999). In other words, the ZPD is constantly unfolding and is more an attribute of the situation in which one learns (e.g. by interacting with experts around a real task) than an attribute of individuals.

window treatments and to activate schema about redecorating their home. When the second statement—"Goose hunting season opens soon"—is revealed, the reader must recognize that she activated the incorrect schema. It is interesting that in Wisconsin and Maine—where bird hunting is common—many people do initially activate the hunting schema because this is "close to home." In other parts of the country, this rarely happens. This demonstrates how we naturally apply and build meaning from our past experience. Now try this one:

She ran quickly toward the rising sun

This statement often stimulates readers to begin visualizing a female jogger doing her morning workout or a girl running down the beach toward her lover. When they read "knowing fresh oats would be in the barn," they must bring a new set of schematic knowledge of horses and barnyards to bear as they revise what they envision. If they do not have any experience with or schema knowledge of farms, then they will not be able to envision this revised meaning. One boy in this situation told me in response, "They must be serving oatmeal in the barn." He did not have the requisite schema to correctly envision the sentence.

So where *is* the meaning when we read? Is it totally *in the text*? If this were the case, all readers would discern the same meaning, but as we see above, they do not. Is the meaning totally *in the reader's head*? If this were the case, we could not say that my student was wrong about a jogger eating Quaker oatmeal in the barn after her run. Or is meaning created somewhere *between* the reader's knowledge and needs and the verbally coded information offered by the text? It is obvious to me, from examples such as these and from my research with adolescent readers, that reading is a transaction that requires a conversation between a reader, her schema, and the text.

Consider this example:

> I walk around the house all day
> Run through the yard
> And help with play
> When nighttime falls
> I find my place and
> Underneath the bed I'll stay

In this case, the reader needs not only to activate conceptual/topical schematic knowledge (of shoes) but schematic knowledge of genre (the text type *riddle*) and procedures (appropriate strategies—seeing complex implied relationships). Recognizing the text as a riddle helps us to activate the proper interpretive operations. We have to recognize the tip-off for the game we are in, and we have to know the rules of the game: We must see the common thread across deliberately mysterious cues to identify what is being described. If we don't know that this is what riddles ask us to do, we'll have to build our schema by being taught these rules and strategic moves before we can be successful with this text and others that are like it.

Recognizing that this poem is a riddle means that we know we must solve the riddle. It also means we must know to do so by matching the description provided metaphorically (through personification) with an inanimate object that is quite tangentially described and is unnamed.

If students possess the conceptual/topical, genre/text type, and procedural/strategic knowledge they need, then we need to help them activate this background. We need to help them to notice the conventional tip-offs that tell them they must activate such knowledge. For example, with the riddle they must recognize that they are being asked to complete the metaphor and then "fill in the blank" of the comparison. If they do not possess the requisite schematic knowledge, we must teach them this knowledge before they begin to read a text that requires it. Only learning-centered theories fully recognize—and emphasize—that students need to be helped to know *how* to read new kinds of texts (e.g., fables, extended definitions, classifications, ironic monologues) as well as textual conventions (e.g., irony or symbolism). In teacher-centered approaches, students are taught by being lectured, assigned tasks, and evaluated on their performance; in student-centered ones, by engaging with the texts on their own.

Schema
Unique as a Fingerprint

As Gambrell and Koskinen (2002) point out in their excellent review, it is important for the teacher to understand that students' spontaneous use of imagery will be individual and unique, shaped by their personal experiences and background knowledge. If you ask students to imagine a wristwatch, for instance, some may imagine an analog watch with hands, others a digital watch with flashing numbers, some a Mickey Mouse watch, and still others a Swatch. There is a direct relationship between a student's experiential background and both comprehension and imagery, since students must draw on their experience to comprehend and create images. If students do not have those resources, they must be provided the requisite experiences—with photographs, movies, objects, labs, drama work, field trips, and so on before they read.

Teachers and students both need to understand that while there are no absolutely right or wrong ways of imagining a text, and that their images will be unique and idiosyncratic, there *are* valid and invalid images. The best and most valid images are those that combine personal background experience with direct and implied cues from a text to create a visualization that is consistent with and respectful of all the details of a text's coded construction. These are the kinds of images that best promote textual comprehension.

GOOD TEACHING IS SEQUENCED

No matter what the content we're teaching, we need to sequence our teaching so that it starts where students currently are and guides and leads them to where they need to be. This book will explore how to use visualization strategies in such sequences. The following model demonstrates what I mean by a sequential process of teaching; see chapter five for a fuller discussion of it.

PRE-ASSESS: IDENTIFY STUDENTS' NEEDS

1. The teacher ascertains which strategies students need but don't yet know how to use. This can be done through pre-assessments using think-alouds, action strategies, visuals, and so forth.

MODELING: I DO/YOU WATCH

2. The teacher models the use of a challenging new strategy in the context where it is needed, and the students watch.

SHARING EXPERTISE: I DO/YOU HELP

3. The teacher uses the strategy, citing the tip-off in the text that signals the need, and activates the interpretive operations. She asks the students to help out by citing subsequent tip-offs, and talking the teacher's way through the strategy.

GRADUAL RELEASE: YOU DO TOGETHER/I HELP

4. Students work together in small groups to find the tip-offs and practice using the required strategy.

ASSESSING MASTERY: YOU DO/I WATCH

5. Finally, individual students use the strategy independently. If they cannot, they continue working in groups or with the help of the teacher. The important thing is for the student to get the right amount of support to be successful—to move through the ZPD (to a new ZAD.)

These are the steps I used with Curtis and the process that I propose that you use with all students. It comprises a form of what is known as scaffolding— providing very explicit and active assistance in handing over expert knowledge that helps students to master new strategies. I use several elaborated versions of this model throughout this book.

Scaffolding for a particular strategy can be applied in different ways to meet the different needs of various students in your classroom. For example, I might continue working with small groups of struggling students as they watch me use the strategy and then try to help me use it. Students who are getting it but still need some help work together. I'll drop in when I can to help. And those who

"Any person who is intellectually alive changes his ideas. If anyone at a university is teaching the same thing they were teaching five years ago, either the field is dead, or they haven't been thinking."

Noam Chomsky, New York Times Magazine
Interview with Deborah Solomon, 11/2/03

can use the strategy independently can work at applying it on their own, or perhaps I'll find a more complicated textual challenge for using the strategy that they can address in small groups or on their own. In this way, everybody gets pushed and scaffolded appropriately to grow as far as they can.

Scaffolding itself is a very powerful metaphor for good teaching, so powerful I would like to pay some attention to this metaphor and the research around it.

Wood, Bruner and Ross (1976) were the first researchers to use this metaphor as they described how mothers guide their young children to develop language.

These researchers demonstrated that parents who were successful scaffolders:

- took advantage of real situations in which language could be developed and applied with real consequences—they taught in real contexts at the point of need;

- considered the child's interests, goals, and current abilities;

- focused the child's attention on the task at hand;

- kept them motivated to work on the task;

- modeled successful completion of the task, as often as necessary;

- encouraged the child to participate in helping them complete the task, if the child could not do it alone;

- divided tasks into manageable chunks, so that success was attainable;

- kept the task at the appropriate level of difficulty (in the child's zone of proximal development);

- lent help and expertise at the point of need when necessary for the child to successfully complete the task;

- offered a variety of support "customized" to the current needs of the child in the current situation—they used not just one boilerplate method but constantly experimented and varied their approach;

- used feedback from observing the child to inform subsequent instruction—their teaching was responsive and reciprocal, and the child provided feedback about what worked and didn't work and therefore how she needed to be taught;

- introduced new tasks to provide a constant state of challenge, continually "upping the ante" by asking for more sophisticated responses ("fah" might be accepted for fish, then "fishy," but children were never allowed to backslide and were continually challenged to be more specific, expert, and precise);

- directed attention to relevant features of the task and developed situationally-based strategies for dealing with these features;

- eventually asked the child to complete the task on her own, but only when this could be done with a probability of success.

The goal of such scaffolding is for the learner to internalize mental functions, such as mastering spoken language or reading strategies, so that these can be independently used. But achieving this goal requires sensitive, persistent, and relational teaching. It is not easy work. The standard placed on the accomplished teacher for providing scaffolding is a high one.

Purposeful Learning and Reading
Macro and Micro-Purposes

The last point I want to make in this chapter is that scaffolding must serve both macro and micro purposes. In other words, whatever we teach has to resonate outside the classroom. And we have to let our students know that it will—that whatever it is they are sweating over is useful knowledge they can transfer to their lives outside of school. The issue of transfer is central to education: If we do not teach students something during a class that they can then use in their next class or in their lives, then we have taught them nothing.

Why raise the bar so high? Because while teacher-centered theories are oriented toward the *past*, and established sets of information, and student-centered theories are focused on the *present*, on what the student is interested in and can do now, learning-centered teaching and scaffolding are *future-oriented*. They are focused on what the student can do next. It is an instructional style that seeks to build specific strategies and capacities among groups of students and among individuals. Because of this future orientation, scaffolding requires clear goals, a clear focus on actual tasks, and lots of assistance to help students make each new leap into the possibilities of the future.

DEFINING OUR GOALS

I've argued that inquiry is the most powerful way to conceive of curriculum and teaching (See Hillocks, 1995; 1999; Wilhelm, 1997; Wilhelm and Friedemann, 1998; Wilhelm and Edmiston, 1998; Smith and Wilhelm, 2002, Beach and Myers, 2002; et al for data-driven arguments for this position). In fact, I've argued that reading and writing are best thought of as forms of inquiry and best taught in the context of inquiry (See also, Wilhelm, forthcoming).

We've seen that every content area is a community of practice. This community can be considered a field of inquiry which produces and uses knowledge. Knowing what strategies expert practitioners in science or math make use of can help us to apprentice our "novice experts," so that they can read and think with the same kind of intellectual tools.

Every activity we give our students should serve an overarching goal. I want my students to be skilled enough to exercise choices in their lives and flexibly apply strategies to new situations.

Once we understand the kinds of seminal tasks to be engaged, we can identify the strategic demands of these tasks and consider how to build an instructional sequence—or a scaffold of activities—that will help students to develop the necessary skills over time, text by text and activity by activity, as they climb the ladder towards expertise. To do this, we need specific teaching goals.

First, I need macro goals, or global goals. My own macro goal is to help my students become independent readers, writers, problem-solvers, and learners, so that they can exercise choices in their lives and serve community interests by being active, democratic citizens. My awareness of this goal helps me ask how what I am doing each day serves this global end. If my instruction does not serve this end, I can ask how it can be amended to better do so. What issues are my students and I inquiring into; what knowledge and functions do I hope they will master and apply? What is the ultimate "end" of my teaching?

Likewise, I need micro goals and micro scaffolds at the local level of daily instruction and minute-by-minute interactions with particular kids. How is my lesson-by-lesson work serving my global ends and the ultimate goals of our inquiry or unit? I need to understand the task at hand, and how the assistance I provide will help students to develop strategies for meeting the goals and completing the tasks.

SKATING WITH MY FRIEND GARY

My friend Gary Feight is a consummate teacher. One of his favorite things to teach is ice hockey skating. I've often seen him take a child struggling to skate and transform him or her into an incredibly powerful skater. I've watched him teach several times under the glaring halogen lights above the glaze of ice at the West Bend hockey rink. And I've seen him use scaffolding intelligently when he teaches.

The first comment Gary makes to a new student is "I've got to learn you before I can teach you." So he gets to know his new charges, discovering their motivations for learning to skate and the state of their current abilities. After chatting for a while, he'll ask his student to take some turns around the rink, saying, "You skate and I'll follow." Gary is typically attired in his brown canvas coat and a black wool hat that looks like a skullcap, since it appears to be a size too small. He'll skate behind his student and ask him to do some stops and other moves. He'll watch carefully and nod to himself, taking mental note of exactly what the student does and doesn't do. From this, Gary learns what the student can do (zone of actual development) and therefore what she can do next with his help (zone of proximal development).

Gary tells me, "You have to start by making kids feel good, by showing them they already have some skill and ability and therefore the potential for future success. Then you show them how you can build from their current competence to continued growth."

When Gary teaches a new move, he'll say, "I'll skate, you follow" (I Do/You Watch). Then he typically gives his students drills to practice the skills involved. Quite often he makes the moves as he tows them or guides them along (I Do/You Help or You Do/ I Help). His younger students love it when he goes full-bore with them in tow to give them the feel of particular moves, then turns and abruptly stops, ice chips flying into the air. There's a lot of laughter and chatter during Gary's lessons. "How did that feel?" he asked one young boy after towing him around the rink twice. "Holy cow!" the boy replied. "Will I ever be able to skate that fast?" "Ha!" Gary laughed. "In a year you'll think that what we just did was in slow motion, like molasses in the freezer!" The boy shakes his head and smiles in disbelief.

After teaching a technique, Gary then has a student try it independently and in a real situation (YOU DO/I WATCH), such as in a hockey scrimmage. Gary has shown me that teaching in such a relational and scaffolded manner ultimately leads to independence—to students literally "skating away" on their own.

This is what we want for our students as readers, and this is what we explore in the next chapter: using the concreteness of visualization to scaffold our students up, up, and away into more heightened forms of reading.

CHAPTER 3

Using Our Lives to See What We Read

Introductory Visualization Techniques

When my seventh graders arrived each day, I required them to show me the reading materials they had brought to class, give me a high five, and say "I am a reader!" or "I love reading!" or "Reading class rocks!" It was a fun ritual for most, but not for Marko. Each day he'd give me a high five and say something along the lines of "Reading is stupid!" or, on bad days, "Reading is for wusses!" Marko had one of the toughest shells I've ever had to crack. When I'd ask him to describe what he was seeing as he read, he couldn't do it. Working one-on-one with him, I discovered that he even had difficulty perceiving the actual words on the page. For example, when I asked him to tell me what he saw in a book about the Revolutionary War, he replied, "Just a bunch of black squiggles, like rabbit poop on the snow!"

We cannot read what we cannot see. This means students need to be able to perceive words *and* build visual meanings based on the ideas words communicate and suggest to us.

It was then I realized that Marko was absolutely right in declaring that reading was stupid; for him, it was. To help Marko, I had to dig deep to help him "see" the actual words he was reading and then assist him in visualizing from these words. He didn't seem to have the vaguest notion of the end goal of reading—comprehending and making powerful meaning with text. I was badly out of my depth. I had to stretch my teaching repertoire, looking to both Marko and to various experts for ideas about how to help him. It was tough going, but in concert with some teachers who knew more than I did, Marko helped me to become a better teacher—one who could help him to become a better reader.

At the suggestion of our learning disabilities (LD) specialist, Judy Bovee, I asked our shop teacher to make a desktop sandbox in which both Marko and I could trace letters and words with our fingertips. I also brought in string that we used to create letters and words. These processes seemed remarkably helpful in getting Marko to perceive unknown words and to be able to pronounce them, perhaps because they helped him to "see" the phonemes from which the words were made. But this was only the start. For the words to be meaningful, we now had to work on visualizing the meaning indicated by them. To this end, Marko and I sketched or acted out the meanings of words and phrases, created pictorial flash cards and grab bags, and engaged in many other visual activities.

Throughout our work together, I used the sociocultural scaffolding scheme of I DO/YOU WATCH, I DO/YOU HELP, YOU DO/I HELP, YOU DO/I WATCH. Because Marko was keen on car repair, we renamed the steps of this process as follows:

Finding Our Bearings
Getting Our Hands Dirty
Making and Fixing It Together
Doing It on My Own

Marko had struggled for so long; I wanted to communicate that I would be with him every step of the way until he was ready to work on his own. For this reason, we focused on the "our" until he was ready for independence.

Marko was sometimes rambunctious and resistant, and our sessions often did not run smoothly. But after a semester of intense work, Marko was showing visible improvement as a reader. He certainly had a new understanding of what reading was and of himself as a reader, as evidenced by the fact that he often gave up lunch period for help with his reading. He also began to bring his reading materials to class, something he had resolutely refused to do earlier in the year. I realized that his resistance had been rooted in his feeling that he would never get the help he needed to become a reader. Once I convinced him that I would not give up on him, he began to show some enthusiasm for the project of learning to read. This was not a boy who resisted literacy. This was a boy who resisted failure and was angry about the lack of assistance available to him.

In this chapter, I share some easy ways to get started with visualization strategies, whether you're teaching challenging students like Marko or proficient readers. I focus first on some of the word-level techniques that are effective for struggling readers, then proceed to techniques for helping students of all abilities to comprehend larger chunks of text.

Visualizing from Words
Suggested Activities

A basic ability for all readers, from elementary through high school, is the capacity to visualize the meanings of concepts or individual words. A scheme posed by the work of Fredericks (1986) and Barclay (1990) and based on the seminal work of Sadoski (1985) on visualization can help readers to achieve this. (Cf. a helpful summary of these schemes is provided in Gambrell and Koskinen, 2002.)

The seven-step sequence below is especially helpful to students at all ages and grade levels who, like Marko, may not yet be able to visually imagine at the word and local levels. For them, start with step one. For more accomplished readers, start later in the sequence, at their point of need.

Either in a whole class setting or small groups, prompt students to:

1. **Create mental images of observed concrete objects.** Bring in interesting objects and have students handle, study, and carefully observe each object. Then have them close their eyes and imagine the most detailed version of the object that they can. Prompt them to describe the item to their classmates; other students can chime in with details they would add or change. Finally, have students open their eyes and compare their mental pictures and descriptions with the actual object they were attempting to imagine, noting how their vision and the object are similar and different. Emphasize that good readers use observed objects and visual experiences from their lives to form images as they read.

2. **Create elaborate mental images of imagined concrete objects.** Now ask students to visualize an absent concrete object with which they have previous experience. Next, use guided imagery prompts to have them create ever more detailed visions of this object. For example, you could ask students to imagine a car, then provide additional specific details to get students to refine their visualization. You might prompt them to see a red sports car, or a red Corvette (just remember to choose something students

are familiar with, if you want them to be that specific), a shiny red Corvette glistening with rain, a Corvette that is a convertible, with the top down, with white leather seats, and with its lights flashing. The point is to prompt students to move from imagining recently seen objects to visualizing objects by retrieving images from memory, and then refining and adapting these visions based on verbal cues. This prepares students to respond to cues in texts while reading and to continue to refine and build these images based on new and accumulating detail. This skill is an essential one that is gained by bringing visual experiences from one's life to the reading.

3. **Envision familiar objects and settings from their own experience.** Next, prompt students to imagine familiar objects or scenes from home, such as the sugar jar in the kitchen, a clock, their bedroom, or a favorite place in their neighborhood. Invite them to sketch pictures and take them home to compare them to the actual objects or scenes, amending the drawings or adding details to them as they wish. You might also prompt students to use their perception of a bedroom or house and revise it to create a vision of a house or bedroom they have never seen, by using the kinds of prompts described in step 2.

4. **Add familiar actions and events, then relationships and settings.** Ask students to envision a familiar event or action, like a tea kettle whistling, or to run a brief video clip they have seen back through their mind. Then ask them to build on an imagined object, such as the car described in step 2, by visualizing it in a driveway on a sunny day, then pulling out of the driveway, squealing its wheels as it peels out, and stopping at a stop sign. Visualization skills are extended when students describe the relationship of the object to other objects or characters or put the object in motion or in a situation. The more sophisticated they become at envisioning, the more their visions will move and involve these kinds of relationships.

5. **Picture characters, settings, details, and events while listening to a story read or told aloud.** Read aloud imagery-intense narrative and expository

informational text (be sure to read both!) about events, settings, processes, or ideas that are familiar to students so that they will have images from their recent experiences to draw on as resources. Stop periodically to ask students to share their mental pictures; you might even ask them to identify what experiences they drew on to create their images. To extend this activity, have students work individually or in groups to create illustrations for each section of text (see chapter 6).

6. **Study text illustrations and use them to create internal images.** Discuss text illustrations of all kinds with students as you read with them. Discuss how illustrations work in various ways to give readers a sense of setting or context (see chapter 6), characters, concepts, mood, interactions, relationships, actions, events, and trends. Explain that narratives ask us to visualize a world and expository texts often ask us to create a mental model of a map, graph, or process (more on this in chapter 5). Think aloud about how you use such figures and illustrations to create your own mental pictures and models, and how you then use these mental representations to remember and think with. Prompt students to use text illustrations in the same ways. Explain that even when text illustrations are not available, their task as readers is to create the same kinds of visuals that would help them understand and manipulate textual ideas.

7. **Create mental pictures independently.** Prompt students to create mental pictures as they read on their own. (If students cannot do this, work with them using prior activities in this seven-step sequence.) I've found it effective to invite students to create journal entries or drawings that respond to prompts I provide at strategic points in a text.

Remember that you might choose to start at different points of this sequence with different students, depending on what they already do as readers. More engaged readers might only need step seven, but readers who struggle will benefit from the whole sequence. Once a student "gets it," move on to challenge him or her in another way by using ideas from a subsequent step.

ESPECIALLY FOR STRUGGLING READERS

Nanci Bell (1991) provides a particularly effective scheme to assist struggling readers, one that is consistent with the seven-step sequence. She argues that an essential part of reading is the ability to create a "Gestalt," or a visual sense of a whole scene, idea, or plot progression. Her findings are in line with my own classroom data (Wilhelm, 1995, 1997): Highly engaged, successful readers see details, ideas, and scenes and are able to blend these together into an organic and dynamic whole. This synthesizing process has many benefits for the reader. Bell cites Long, Winograd, and Bridge (1989):

> Imagery may be involved in the reading process in a number of ways. First, imagery may increase the capacity of working memory during reading by assimilating details and propositions into chunks which are carried along during reading. Second, imagery seems to be involved in making comparisons or analogies—that is, in matching schematic and textual information. Third, imagery seems to function as an organizational tool for coding and storing meaning from the reading. (Bell, 1991, pg. 250)

In Bell's scheme, students are helped to visualize the meaning represented by written words. They are assisted, one on one, in moving from "word imaging" to "single sentence imaging" to "sentence by sentence imaging" with oral and then written language. Eventually, students are assisted in handling multiple-sentence imaging, whole-paragraph imaging, and paragraph-by-paragraph imaging. A unique part of Bell's program is the use of "structure word" prompts. As a resource for creating rich visions, readers use cards with prompts, like *what*, *where*, and *when*, as well as more specific words, like *size*, *shape*, *movement*, and synesthetic elements, like *mood*. Students refer to the cards while visualizing to help them refine their visualization.

READING IS SEEING

Bell's research involved intense treatment: four hours of daily work with students for a total of nearly 48 hours. She established that this intense work resulted in statistically significant increases in comprehension for readers from elementary school to retirement age. Her book *Visualizing and Verbalizing* (1991) is highly recommended by my colleagues in special education, who have used her technique to great effect.

ACTIVITIES FOR WORD-LEVEL VISUALIZATION

Students who have great difficulty perceiving individual words and stitching them together to comprehend a text's meaning benefit from individual and small-group work with the activities listed below. Notice that these activities are ways of localizing and intensifying the work described in step one of the seven-step sequence I have described earlier.

WRITING IN SAND OR WITH STRING.

Have students trace words in a small sandbox or give them string, clay, and pipe cleaners and have them form words with these materials. These two techniques were remarkably successful with Marko. Judy Bovee, the learning specialist who recommended them to me, felt that Marko was so profoundly LD that he needed a visual and kinesthetic experience of words before he would remember and recognize them. Young children are often given these tactile experiences; teachers of older struggling readers aren't as likely to know about these techniques.

DRAWING WORD REPRESENTATIONS.

When students have difficulty imagining a particular noun or verb, it is often helpful to ask them to visualize a noun or verb that is familiar to them. You can then ask them specific questions about attributes, such as color, size, context, motion, effect, or emotion, until you can draw the specific picture they are envisioning. Build on this by giving students the information they need to visualize the meaning of an

CONSIDER THIS

Rudolf Arnheim, a pioneer of visual psychology, asserts that behind every word is some kind of image. The history of written language began with pictographs that drew on this direct relationship. In English we use the "phonetic rebus" principle, which allows us to use symbols for their phonetic value. But students can still use the intimate connection between words and images to help them comprehend and create meaning with words.

> **NEBULA** — *Stellar Life Forms*
>
> – Nebulae are clouds of gas and/or dust in interstellar space. Nebulae can be seen when they glow, which is called emission Nebulae – by scattering light from within them – reflection nebulae – by blocking light from stellar objects from behind them – obscuration nebulae

A picture flash card of the term *nebula*.

unfamiliar word until they can make a drawing that captures the central meaning of that word.

PICTURE FLASH CARDS.

Ask students to write a word on one side of an index card. On the other side, have them draw a picture or use a clip art image that in some way captures the word's meaning. Ask students to explain how their image connects to the word's meaning. To extend the activity, have students include a written definition, a synonym, or an antonym of the word.

INFORMATION GAP ACTIVITY

In this activity, one student knows something that his or her classmates do not, and this student is asked to convey what he or she knows to others. I learned of this concept from Karl Androes of Chicago's Reading in Motion, who came across it in *Games for Language Learning* by Andrew Wright, David Bettridge and Michael Buckby. It's a great way to add suspense to language lessons. For example, in Karl's dance-based work with younger students on phonemic awareness and the alphabetic principle, the teacher whispers a word or nonsense word into the ear of a student (or to a small group), who is designated as the performer. The performer's task is to figure out what letters represent the spoken sounds of that word and how to make those letter shapes with his body in order to spell the word correctly. The performer then performs the word for the rest of the class, who must guess what word the performer is spelling. Students love trying to be the first to guess the word. This activity can also be used to portray concepts, ideas, and scenes through illustrating the meaning or aspects of the term.

Vocabulary tableau: Students perform the meaning of the word *oppression*.

VOCABULARY TABLEAUX.

Jamie Heans, a teacher in Brewer, Maine (the PDN site where I worked for several years), uses this and the following two techniques to teach new vocabulary. Tableau is the French word for "visual presentation," so a "vocabulary tableau" is a visual presentation of a relevant vocabulary word. A vocabulary tableau might be a mural, a chalk drawing on the board, or a pose or dance. Students might be asked to create a simple statue or a statue with a commentary or epitaph to illustrate a word. Or they might create a moving statue, photograph, or short video clip (which is particularly useful in describing an action or process). Jamie often assigns student groups to "perform" different vocabulary terms. For example, for a unit on survival, students might perform the meaning of the term *symbiosis* by showing a group working together, or perform the word *niche* by having one student occupy a space no one else enters as they go about their business around the first student. (See chapter 6; and Wilhelm, 2002)

VOCABULARY POWERPOINT.

Jamie sometimes asks his students to create quick PowerPoint slides of vocabulary words, having them illustrate word meanings through clip art, photographs found in magazines or taken with a digital camera, embedded video (found or created), animation, and music. PowerPoint and its equivalents (like Apple's Keynote) are very simple forms of presentation software that many kids already know how to use or can learn within a class period. I have watched Jamie's students create vocabulary and terminology slides in less than ten minutes. A slide show of the whole class' efforts can be created and shared within a 40-minute period and made available as an electronic reference or glossary throughout a unit.

VIDEO CLIPS FOR SUMMARIZING.

Students often have difficulty grasping the basic facts of a story or text and then putting these into the right sequence or another kind of meaningful pattern. To help your students build this vital skill, have them create short videos of the major scenes or ideas of a text in a meaningful sequence. Encourage them to make their video summaries as brief as possible—this activity is meant to be quick, easy, and somewhat spontaneous.

Michael Smith's Rules for Drama work:
- Short
- Scriptless
- Spontaneous
- Not Seldom

VIDEO CLIPS FOR EXPLORING LITERARY DEVICES.

Assign small student groups a literary device and a scene from a book the class is reading. Each group's task is to create a video that defines the device, then displays the technique in action in a scene they have read. Videos conclude with a commentary on how the device helps to create meaning. For example, I recently watched a group of Jamie's students make a video defining the term *soliloquy* during a single class period. They did so with great humor, first querying two students about the

> "The next student fabricated a definition, claiming that a soliloquy was a rare African silkworm."

meaning of the term. One said, "Uhhh…I really have absolutely no idea." The next student fabricated a definition, claiming that a soliloquy was a rare African silkworm. Then the group inserted a clip that reads "Actually…" and offering the correct definition. They then performed a scene with a person speaking thoughts aloud as if no one else could hear and explained that a soliloquy helps readers to understand a scene by allowing them to read or hear the character's thoughts. When the class had finished the book they were working on, they compiled their work into a video glossary of literary terms that included how the terms were put to use by the author. This is one of my favorite visualization activities, because kids are so highly engaged by it and often create hilarious or poignant movies. And because the videos are shown to the rest of the class as soon as they are made, they enhance the discussion of the text and boost every reader's understanding.

GAMES.

Games like Pictionary™ or Cranium™, which require students to draw ideas, vocabulary, or concepts, are both fun and excellent at stimulating visualization. I have such games in my room and often play one with students during lunch or encourage them to do so during study hall, if they have no homework.

RESOURCES

An excellent resource for helping students to perceive words and their meanings is Kylene Beers's *When Kids Can't Read: What Teachers Can Do* (Heinemann, 2002). Thomas Armstrong's *The Multiple Intelligences of Reading and Writing* (ASCD, 2003) also provides many supportive strategies for helping students perceive, experience, and make meaning with words.

Techniques for Visualizing
Across Text

Of course, being able to comprehend and visualize word meanings and central concepts is essential to reading. As necessary as this skill is, by itself it is not sufficient for achieving an expert level of reading. Students must learn to coherently envision chunks of text as organic meanings.

Therefore, in addition to using many of the ideas cited above, I also took care to do a lot of reading to and for Marko, then with him, before I asked him to read on his own. I usually read a text to him and then used the activities above to do "word work" with a few vocabulary words from the reading. This helped him to remember that the skills we were learning were not decontextualized but should be put to use in real reading situations to make meaning, and that the ultimate end of our project was for him to be able to read on his own.

While I was working with Marko, who was a big sports fan, I brought in the newspaper every day and we read the sports page together. This had a huge unintended benefit. As we often read about sporting events that Marko had attended or games he had watched on TV, he was assisted in visualizing the scenes and events described in the stories: He could use his memory of actually seeing the events instead of having to imagine them from scratch. Also, instead of feeling that Marko's attendance at sports events and his television viewing were taking away from his study time, I was able to use it as a resource to help him improve as a reader. I also taught Marko how to search the Internet, and we bookmarked several Milwaukee Brewers, Green Bay Packers, and Wisconsin Badgers websites on which we could monitor stories about his favorite teams.

These activities gave me a sense of déjà vu. I was helped

While it sounds a bit like a template for a blues song, this mnemonic is a way to think about how to gradually release responsibility for using a new strategy to students.

Aloud: Use and model the technique for students. Do it by reading aloud and making the technique visible.

Along: Then do it along with students.

Alone: When they are ready, ask them to do it alone, but be ready to help.

through some reading difficulties myself in second grade by one of the greatest teachers I have ever known. His name was Orlando Schultz, and he claimed that he "could teach anybody to read through one interest." Orlando often taught kids to read with the newspaper by having them follow stories or issues that were of passionate interest to them. And this is what I found myself doing with Marko: teaching him a foundational set of strategies in reading by using the sports he was so interested in.

With Marko, as I would with other struggling readers, I moved from read-alouds and guided imagery with texts we read and re-read together (shown to have significant benefits at all grade levels and with all abilities of students; see Sulzby, 1985) to providing visual prompts with reading we did together or that he did on his own. This allowed him to practice becoming adept at using imagery in independent reading situations.

PUSHING BEYOND PROMPTS

Various studies have demonstrated that simply suggesting to students that they attempt to form visual images as they read improves engagement, comprehension, and comprehension monitoring for many students. It seems that most younger readers do not spontaneously employ imagery as a reading strategy, and yet many have the capacity to do so when prompted (cf., Gambrell and Koskinen, 2002). However, my own studies (Wilhelm 1995; 1997) and those of others, have found that struggling readers do not employ imagery and do not know how to do so. Simply prompting them will not suffice. These readers need scaffolded assistance with visualization strategies. Even more accomplished readers can improve their visualization skills through scaffolded help, which deepens their engagement, comprehension, and ability to learn and use ideas.

It is therefore important to explicitly identify the use of visual strategies to create mental imagery as an essential part of reading. It helps readers to experience stories and other textual information and think about the content of the text.

As you read aloud, identify the cues you use to create a "story world."

READ-ALOUDS AND THINK-ALOUDS TO MODEL IMAGERY (I DO/YOU WATCH)

Reading aloud to students is a great way to help them build their image-making abilities. As you read aloud, be sure you also think aloud to model how you create images as you read. Use texts that are rich in images, and then demonstrate several times how you create images. Below is an example of how I think aloud during read aloud. I often teach a unit on civil rights around the question: What are civil rights, and how can we protect them? One of my favorite texts to use in this unit is *Leon's Story* by Leon Walter Tillage (1997). It's a fabulous story and has beautiful collage art by Susan Roth. Her images symbolize the meaning of Leon's various experiences. This kind of thematic visualization is very helpful to students wrestling with the deep implications of Leon's story. It gives me an opportunity to think aloud about the illustrations and their relationship to the story's meaning, and it gives my students a model of how to use visuals to reinforce thematic implications. This is how I start:

Okay, is everybody on page five of Leon's Story? I look at this collage and I think, it's just row after row of corn. Wow, that must be a lot of work to farm. There's just corn everywhere. It makes me think that maybe Leon's life as a sharecropper was just working in the fields with no time for anything else. In fact, the corn looks like prison bars.

All right, on page seven, let's read together: "We lived on a farm owned by Mr. Johnson. He had lots of acres and grew lots of different crops—corn, tobacco, cotton, alfalfa, wheat, and sometimes sugarcane. It was mostly cotton and tobacco though, because in those days those were the number one crops."

In my mind, I see this big farmhouse where Mr. Johnson lives. I see it as well kept and painted white with black shutters and a big front porch with a swing. I imagine this because Leon says Mr. Johnson owned the farm, and because I grew up on a farm I can use the farmhouses I know to imagine what Mr. Johnson's might look like. In my mind, surrounding the house are fields as far as you can see, full of corn with tassles, big-leafed tobacco plants, and cotton with the cotton balls at the end of branches. I can see all this because these are the crops Leon mentions,

Leon's Story

LEON WALTER TILLAGE
Collage art by Susan L. Roth

Sharecropping

We lived on a farm owned by Mr. Johnson. He had lots of acres and grew lots of different crops—corn, tobacco, cotton, alfalfa, wheat, and sometimes sugarcane. It was mostly cotton and tobacco, though, because in those days those were the number one crops.

My father was a sharecropper, which means he had to share half of everything he had with Mr. Johnson. So, let's say Mr. Johnson gave my father ten acres of tobacco, ten

7

Build a collection of books that have powerful visuals.

because I know what cornfields look like, and because I was once in the south and saw cotton and tobacco farms. I know tobacco looks like this (I draw a picture) and cotton plants look like this (I draw a picture). If I hadn't seen the plants before, I would try to imagine what they might look like.

I also see the decrepit house Leon says they live in: no paint, grey, sagging roof and porch. I also see an aerial view of the farm and how these shacks are spread around at the edge of Mr. Johnson's fields. I think I get the images of the shacks from WPA photographs I have seen. I often use photos or movies I know to help me see what I am reading. And if I don't remember any images, I might try to find some photos on the Internet (With my digital projector, I show them some photos from the WPA and Smithsonian collections). You can do a quick Google search on the Internet and get help visualizing scenes you might not know much about. (I draw a quick sketch of Mr. Johnson's big house, surrounded by crops and, at the edges, little shacks for the sharecroppers.)

Okay, let's continue reading: "My father was a sharecropper, which means he had to share half of everything with Mr. Johnson. So let's say Mr. Johnson gave my father ten acres of corn—whatever—to work. Then, at the end of year, when it came time to sell the crops and settle up, Mr. Johnson would get five acres of each crop and my father would get the other five."

You know, now I am thinking of the collage that started this chapter and how much corn there was. I'm thinking about how much work it must have taken to plant, and to harvest, and then to cut down the stalks and clear the fields. And I take half of the harvest away—but none of the work. I see a bar graph in my mind. One bar is the amount of corn ten acres would produce. Below it is another bar that is half as long, which is the corn Leon and his father would get. (I draw my graph on the board, labeling each line). This is called making a mental model of the meaning of what you are reading. Okay, back to Leon:

"Maybe it sounds good, but the problem was my father had to pay Mr. Johnson for supplies and such, and he purchased the food we'd needed to live on for the past year on credit from the corner store. So out of our half he needed to pay off those debts. . . . At the end of the year, we'd settle our debts. Then Mr. Johnson would say to my father, 'Well, Ivory, you almost got out of debt that time. I think next year you'll make it.'"

In my mind, I see Leon's father giving Mr. Johnson half the corn, then the other half of the corn to pay off his debts, and then Mr. Johnson telling him he is still in debt. I change the graph in my mind so that there is no bar for the corn that Leon and his father would get, and a long bar representing all of the corn going to Mr. Johnson. (I change my graph on the board.) And I see how Leon and his father have done all the work and gotten none of the corn. All they have earned is enough food to survive, and they are still indebted to Mr. Johnson, so they have to keep working for him next year. In my mind, the scene with Mr. Johnson and Leon and his father takes on a red tint because I am sure Leon and his father are being cheated and I am angry about that. Okay, we're going to continue reading, but now I want you to visualize in your mind what you see. I'd like you to be able to tell a partner what words from the text help you to see what Leon describes, and what experiences from your life help you to see it. If you can't see it, think of where you could find some pictures or have some experiences that would help you to see it.

Basic Ways to Conduct Think-Alouds

- Teacher does think-aloud; students listen.

- Teacher does think-aloud; students help out.

- Students do think-alouds as large group; teacher and other students monitor and help.

- Students do think-alouds as small group; teacher and other students monitor and help.

- Individual student does think-aloud in forum; other students help.

- Students do think-aloud individually; compare with others.

- Teacher or students do think-alouds orally, in writing and or pictures, on an overhead, with notes, or in journal.

For more on using the think-aloud strategy, see *Improving Comprehension with Think-Aloud Strategies.*

As you read and think aloud, identify the cues that you use to begin creating a "story world" (for a narrative) or a "mental model" of the information, concepts, or processes (for both narrative and informational text). You might even choose to draw quick sketches of your story world or mental model and share them with students. Be sure to identify the cues that prompted you and the life experiences you used to build the images the way you did. If I can, I provide students with a short excerpt of the text that I will think aloud with and have them circle or underline the visual cues I use to make my mental images. Later on in the process, I ask students to circle their own clues, first with my help, then on their own.

As you do this kind of thinking aloud and visual prompting, you might focus on particular techniques the author uses, conventions of particular kinds of texts (such as classification, argument, and expository writings), or conventions that run across texts (such as symbolism, irony, and unreliable narrators). In my classroom, I use lots of expository texts for read aloud and think aloud—including primary source materials, nonfiction, and historical texts—because these can be challenging for young readers who are used to reading fictional narrative. For example, I might read aloud from great children's or young adult books like *Dolphin Man* (Pringle, 2003) to show how gripping quotes are used to put readers in the midst of the action. *Phineas Gage* (Fleischman, 2002) starts with a description of Phineas using the tamping iron that explodes through his brain but does not kill him or destroy his intellectual functions. The author prompts readers to visualize and live through the incredible scene that was the beginning of modern brain science. Jim Murphy's *Across America on an Emigrant Train* (1993) uses a real diary entry to open each chapter, establishing the historical situation and personal context. When I highlight the features of such texts—including their use of quotation, historical anecdote, and primary source materials—I help students to see how authors use particular techniques to help their audience see and experience what they are reading. In turn, students learn how to craft their own writing to shape the experience of an audience.

READ-ALOUDS AND GUIDED IMAGERY (I DO/YOU HELP)

The next step is to induce students to create images is to prompt them as they listen to you read either stories or informational text. Instead of creating or describing the images yourself, cite the prompts you have noticed and ask students to create and describe their visualizations to the class, small groups, or partners. Provide assistance as needed by asking for justifications based on text cues or by correcting misconceptions, if students bring inconsistent images to bear. Have students compare and contrast the images they have created, and compare the textual cues and life experiences they used to create such images.

It is important when using guided imagery and think-alouds to identify the visual and descriptive cues you use to see what you read. These stimulate image-making, helping students to notice and use these cues on their own.

The research makes it clear both that imagery is an essential part of the expert reader's repertoire and that many students need very explicit and active teacher support to internalize this strategy for themselves. Repeated practice and prompting will help students to develop the skill of creating images based on text cues, and will help them to do this habitually. It is important for us as teachers to stress that valid images depend both on the reader's experience and on textual cues, and that the actual image depends on the active engagement of the reader.

SIMPLE PROMPTING (YOU DO/I HELP)

Eventually, you can read aloud, or have students read aloud to each other, and simply prompt them to circle visual cues and make pictures in their heads about story events or ideas. With some readers, simple prompting will suffice to

TIPS FOR MODELING THE PROMPTS

During a longer reading, stop periodically to share images of characters, events, settings, ideas, key details, and processes, and the clues that helped you create these images.

help them visualize. Using the techniques described in this chapter will help even struggling readers eventually progress to the point where you can simply prompt them, then intervene as necessary. *As always, teaching interventions should be used only if and when needed by particular students or groups of students.* Often, a technique will be helpful to everyone in a class. Sometimes, the level of support or way the technique is used will vary between classroom groups. At other times, perhaps only a few students will require the intervention. It all depends on your students' zones of proximal development. Luckily, all the techniques offered here are flexible and can be pitched to readers at almost any level of expertise. Below are prompts to share with your students.

SOME GENERAL VISUALIZATION PROMPTS:

◆ As you read, make pictures in your mind to help you understand and remember.

◆ Try to build images of people, places, interactions, events, processes, and ideas as you read.

◆ Use memories and objects from your life experience to "see" what you are reading.

◆ Make a movie in your mind as you read.

◆ Try to recall the major scene, main idea, important process, and so on, from your reading by using an image or moving images.

◆ Use visuals to placehold major ideas and their sequence.

◆ Explain how and why visions or pictures develop and change with the introduction of new information.

SOME PROMPTS FOR SEEING THE "STORY WORLD":

◆ What impressions are forming in your mind of the people and settings?

◆ Where did the story take place? What is it like there? What kinds of buildings, trees, and so on, do you see?

◆ Does it matter where the story takes place? Could it have happened elsewhere or anywhere? Does it matter when the story happened? Is the historical situation important or could it have happened anywhere?

◆ Does it matter from what perspective you see the story? How would the story and what you see as the reader be different if it were told from another viewpoint?

◆ How do you respond to the setting as you read? How does it make you feel? How does it compare to what you know?

◆ If you were going to take a picture or make a movie of a particular scene, where in our community would you stage it? What props would you include? What sort of music would you be playing?

◆ What do the characters look like? How are they dressed or groomed? How do they walk, stand, gesture, interact, or display emotions? What classmates or famous actors would you cast for each part and why?

◆ Where are the characters in relationship to each other? To the setting? To objects in the setting? (This gives you the chance to use maps and tableaux.)

◆ What helps you to see pictures of characters, scenes, events, and ideas? How and when does the clarity of your vision change? From what perspective or position are you seeing the story?

◆ What kinds of details help you to envision the story? How are these connected to your life or reading experiences?

♦   What other ways do you see or sense the story world?

♦   If you were to create a symbol or object to represent the mood of this scene what would it be? How would you create a symbol of the deep meaning or theme of the scene? How would you symbolize a message about human behavior that we could use in our lives?

VISUAL THINK-ALOUDS.

A favorite technique of mine is to have students sketch anything they see, think, or feel as they go through a think-aloud of a text (Wilhelm, 2001). I often type an excerpt of text on the left hand side of a sheet and have students draw their responses on the right side, next to the textual cues that stimulated these responses.

At other times I provide students with sheets of paper and ask them to sketch their visualizations at particular points in the story. I sometimes have them do a back-to-back description: I ask them to identify the visual cues and structure-words that helped them to visualize the particular image or scene they sketched. They then list these cues on the back of their

I left New York in May. I had a penknife, a ball of cord, an ax, and $40, which I had saved from selling magazine subscriptions. I also had some flint and steel which I had bought at a Chinese store in the city. The man in the store had showed me how to use it. He had also given me a little purse to put it in and some tinder to catch the sparks. He had told me that if I ran out of tinder, I should burn cloth, and use the charred ashes.

I thanked him and said, "This is the kind of thing that I am not going to forget."

On the train north to the Catskills I unwrapped my flint and steel and practiced hitting them together to make sparks. On the wrapping paper I made these notes.

"A hard brisk strike is best. Remember to hold the steel in the left hand and the flint in the right, and hit the steel with the flint.

"The trouble is the sparks go every which way."

And that *was* the trouble. I did not get a fire going that night, and as I mentioned, this was a scary experience.

A visual think-aloud for *My Side of the Mountain* by Jean Craighead George.

pictures, so the relationship between verbal stimuli and visual response can be seen. In other words, students see how the cues, their experiences, and their resulting visual representations are all connected.

EMBRACING "ALTERNATIVE" TEXTS AND LITERACIES

In the review of studies *Achieving Literacy* (Meek, et al., 1983), Margaret Meek describes how she assisted illiterate seventh graders in becoming engaged readers through the intense one-on-one reading of picture books. Many of my own most reluctant readers can remember neither having picture books read to them nor reading such books. Such texts, of course, directly connect text to images, communicate the idea that reading is a visual experience, and improve facility at creating such images in one's mind. I encourage you to embrace many forms of texts that combine words and pictures and graphics, including graphic

Denali creates a visual think aloud to explore her response to a book.

novels, magazines, journals, websites, multimedia texts, age-appropriate comic books, sophisticated textbooks, and so on.

PICTURE BOOKS.

I often start a unit by reading picture books, even with my middle and high school students. This provides everyone with a successful reading experience, puts them all in the game, and provides a basic shared background experience. During a recent unit on the Great Depression, my middle schoolers read illustrated

A student reads *Out of the Dust* by Karen Hesse.

books, such as Jerry Stanley's magnificent *Children of the Dust Bowl* and Ann Turner's *Dust for Dinner*. Some students, for whom this reading was appropriately challenging, continued to read these sophisticated kinds of picture books and searched the Internet to find information and images (see, for example, www.scs.state.mi.us/history/ museum/ kidstuff/depression/ costlist.html) to create original picture books that could become classroom resources. Other students went on to read Karen Hesse's *Out of the Dust*, Richard Peck's *A Year Down Yonder*, Christopher Paul Curtis's *Bud, Not Buddy* or David Booth's *The Dust Bowl*. Everyone was reading a text that was appropriately challenging, and everyone could participate fully and equally in the classroom project of studying the Depression and answering our inquiry questions about people's experiences of that time. It all began by reading picture books.

OVERLAY MAPS.

During a unit I helped to plan with teachers at the Chicago Teachers Center, Chicago students read Jim Murphy's books *The Blizzard* (a fascinating story of a debilitating blizzard in New York City that led to the establishment of the National Weather Bureau) and *The Great Fire* (see also www.chicagohs.org/fire) as an introduction to how accounts of disasters can vary. Students created an overlay map: a map of Chicago at the time of the fire overlaying a current map of Chicago. They colored in places that burned as they read the story, adding notes or pictures about important places, people, and events as they read about them.

A teacher introduces *The Great Fire* by Jim Murphy.

RESOURCES

Following are some powerful books that make use of visuals:

Avi's futuristic myth *City of Light; City of Dark*

Robert Burleigh's *Into the Air* about the Wright Brothers' first flight

Steven Kellogg's folklore comic book *Mike Fink*

Mordicai Gerstein's *What Charlie Heard* explores visual connections to Charles Ives' music

Jan Greenberg's *Action Jackson* about the artist Jackson Pollock explores how people see

James Rumford's stunning book *Traveling Man*, about a 14th-century Muslim pilgrim who walked 70,000 miles, uses illuminated Arabic verses from the Koran—useful for units on culture, the hero quest, or the human journey.

◆ Lists such as the Orbis Pictus Awards for children's literature and your library media specialist are great resources for finding such books.

WATCHING VIDEO EXCERPTS.

In a listserve discussion, the noted researcher Judith Langer asserted that using videos could assist students in developing what she calls "envisionment-building stances." She explained that some students are so distant from the language, social situation, settings, or other aspects of a written text that they will have great difficulty "stepping into an envisionment"—a prerequisite for all further engagement and reflection on the text. Scaffolding can be provided by using a video to create some visual images, as sense of setting, time period, character, plot, or language that will help students envision the text. Even short clips may be enough to help students envision the written text.

LUNCH CLUB VIDEOS: READING CAPTIONS.

For a couple of years, I invited a group of students who struggled with reading to a lunch club. We munched our sandwiches in my room while we watched video tapes. We'd watch one of their choice, then one of mine (which would be associated with a unit we were pursuing or a book we were reading). The catch was that there was no sound; students had to read the captions at the bottom of the screen. I found this to be a highly engaging way to get them to read text in a manner that was supported by visual images.

WHAT'S AT STAKE

The research on boys and literacy that I conducted with my mentor Michael Smith (Smith and Wilhelm, 2002) has convinced me that we need to use a wide variety of visual and nonvisual popular-culture texts in the classroom to bridge to more traditional forms of text, and to expand our notions of literacy and text. We found that boys rejected the "schoolishness" of school reading, which they saw as totally divorced from the literacy and concerns that they practiced in their own lives. Bringing in popular-culture texts communicated that the class project would both value and include their literacies and allow them to use these literacies as a resource and bridge to developing school literacies. The boys can therefore see a way to bring competence to school literacies that typically cause them difficulty. Such a project also helps us to expand our notion of what counts as a text. The boys were cynical about school because schools place a high and nearly exclusive value—on long texts such as textbooks, novels, and plays when these were unlike the texts they used in their lives, which were increasingly short electronic and multimedia.

Expanding our notions of text and literacy, and then using these wider views to help students gain new literacies, can be powerful, particularly for our most disenfranchised students.

CHAPTER 4

From the Known to the New

Building Background Before and During Reading

I remember well an afternoon in 1987 when I was teaching Tom Wolfe's The Right Stuff to my English class. One boy asked me what Watergate meant. I referred the question to the class. No one responded. "Come on, people!" I cried. "1972, Richard Nixon's resignation, the erased tapes, the Watergate Hotel! Come on! Let's open those memory banks!" Jamie Delikowski raised his hand and said, "Mr. Wilhelm, none of us were born in 1972, so we can't remember any of that." I was stunned, but a quick mathematical calculation showed me that Jamie was right.

Readers are engaged by topics and settings that are familiar.

I've experienced many moments like this, when my students shocked me with what they didn't yet know, as well as many when they amazed me with what they did know. These experiences taught me the importance of teasing out what students know and don't know before starting a unit. Otherwise, time gets wasted and students get frustrated. But it wasn't until Michael Smith and I embarked on our literacy research (Smith and Wilhelm, 2002) that the vital role of accessing and building knowledge prior to reading really sunk in.

Examining boys' reading habits taught us just how powerful the familiar is to engagement and comprehension. For example, the boys from Maine we studied enjoyed or gravitated toward books about Maine or the Maritime provinces. *Lost on a Mountain in Maine* (Fendler, 1978) was a favorite book of many students, who talked about having seen or climbed Mount Katahdin, which helped them connect to and enjoy the book. *The Perfect Storm* (Junger, 1999) and *The Hungry Ocean* (Greenlaw, 2000) were free-reading choices of many of these boys due to their

THE
ASSESSMENT
BONUS

The techniques introduced in this chapter can serve as pre-assessments to help you plan instruction. They reveal what students know and need to know, so you can teach more effectively.

settings on or off the coast of Maine. They enjoyed reading the poems of Maine poet Paul Corrigan from *At the Grave of the Unknown Riverdriver* (1984) because they recognized the places and the activities he described.

These boys were passionate about the issue of overfishing lobster, a huge debate in that part of the state. They eagerly read *Cod* (Kurlansky, 2003), *The Lobster Chronicles* (Greenlaw, 2002), and many other difficult texts related to this issue. Other boys in the study, whether living in rural, suburban, or urban areas, responded strongly to the familiar, too.

Michael Smith and I were struck by how important geographical locations were to the boys' engagement with reading. To be sure, this finding isn't earthshaking—it's supported by the last 30-plus years of research in cognition—but it resonated with us. The boys we studied embraced books whose terrain was as familiar as the floorboards of their houses or the lobster boats bobbing in the harbor. Put more pedagogically, these books allowed the boys to bring to the text all the details that "connect the dots" and make the text meaningful. They could read with ease, confidence, and enjoyment. In other words, it wasn't just the topics that were compelling; these books were smooth, satisfying rides. They made the boys feel competent as readers because they didn't have to struggle to comprehend them.

We wondered what to do with this finding. How do we as teachers harness the power of the familiar in order to stretch students, to get them to embrace new challenges as readers and thinkers? That's what this chapter explores. In it, I share with you "frontloading" techniques that use visuals to build new images and schema before reading, so that children never come to a text cold. Instead, they'll arrive with a sense of being on familiar terrain, with the resources they need to be successful.

The Benefits
of Frontloading

In terms of the scaffolding metaphor, frontloading lays the foundation of prior experience. New meanings are built on it, and all future learning of more complex versions of the concept depend upon creating a firm foundation. Frontloading techniques accomplish the following:

- They stir children's curiosity about a text;

- They trigger the appropriate background knowledge that students already possess;

- They build and "load up" students' minds with the knowledge they need to comprehend the text.

Frontloading continues throughout a reading until individual students have mastered the independent use of the knowledge. Without it, students' comprehension often collapses, or is never gained in the first place. For example, on one memorable occasion, I was co-teaching a science unit on enzymes. The lead teacher began the unit by having students read the chapter in the textbook. She then gave a quiz on the chapter that nearly everyone in the class failed.

"What went wrong?" she asked me.

"Well," I began, "they don't know anything about enzymes."

"That's why I assigned them the chapter!" she protested. "To introduce them to the basic ideas!"

"But they can't read the text purposefully or comprehend it if they don't know something about enzymes first, or why they should want to know it!"

"Well, how do you ever get started, then?" she asked me.

Trina whispers to Josh the meaning of a good relationship after posting her ideas on a wall chart. Frontloading techniques such as this serve as a gateway to understanding new concepts and strategies. These students were about to launch into a unit on the topic of good relationships.

"We have to give them concrete experiences with enzymes—do experiments, show a filmstrip, talk about enzymes and enzymatic reactions in the home . . ."

After engaging them in these hands-on experiences, our students' interest was much higher and comprehension significantly improved. In fact, the students were able to compose maps and flow charts describing how enzymes work that showed deep understanding.

When I work with teachers, I want them to absolutely remember just a few key things, no matter what. One of them is this: *The most important time to teach reading is before kids read a text that presents them with a new challenge.*

Transactional theories of reading, schema theory, and three decades of cognitive research explain why this is true: The reader must bring meaning to bear on a text in order to be able to comprehend it.

Getting Started
Frontloading Activities

All the frontloading activities presented below are consistent with the Vygotskian injunction that learning must proceed from the known to the new and from the concrete to the abstract. The first is an activity that underlies all of the others and perhaps lives up to Vygotsky and Dewey best of all: providing students with first-hand experiences.

"To perceive, a beholder must create and use his own experience."

— *John Dewey*

Students can be asked to find images about a unit topic before reading. These can be used in frontloading activities like timelines or floorstorming.

FIRST-HAND EXPERIENCES

Research in emergent literacy shows that the most powerful thing we can do to support children in becoming readers is to provide them with life experiences. These life experiences create interests and background knowledge (schema) that empower readers. Introductory field trips, classroom demonstrations, visual aids, drama work, simulations, flow charts, maps, video viewing, and many other experiences are therefore excellent frontloading activities. They provide and build background knowledge students need in order to read particular texts or to pursue thematic inquiries.

In my own experience, field trips and video viewing in schools often have no connection or little connection to what is being studied. It is a shame to waste valuable time and energy that could do powerful work. When I taught in Baltimore, my school began the year with class field trips, which was a great way to build up instructional support for future learning. Each year, I led a group of tenth graders on a bike trip through Civil War sites that took us backwards from the Confederacy's high point to the beginning of the war. We watched the movie *Gettysburg* before we departed. We then followed the route of J.E.B. Stuart's cavalry through Maryland to Gettysburg. Once there, we surveyed the battlefield as if we were Meade's first scouts. We attempted to find strategic advantage. We camped behind the Confederate lines and discussed what our own strategy would have been. The next day, we took a tour of the battlefield, biked the battlelines of each of the battle's three days, and ultimately ran the downhill bayonet charge of the 20th Maine regiment on Little Round Top and walked the route of Pickett's charge. We then biked down to the Antietam battlefield and to the site in Harper's Ferry where Colonel Robert E. Lee captured John Brown. We moved on from there to Manassass, site of the first significant battle of the war.

Upon our return we engaged in a study of politics, power, and history through the American Civil War. We asked: Who tells our stories? Why? How do they influence our thinking? We also explored the flip side: Whose stories are not told, and what do we lose because of this? We read Michael Schaara's *The Killer Angels*, Paul Fleishman's *Bull Run*, and various articles by Garry Wills and others about how Lincoln used the battle and his Gettysburg Address to change the meaning of the war and the meaning of the Constitution, thereby reshaping the future of our nation. The kids used our field trip experiences as a way to think about and make meaning with the texts, and also as a way to understand the influences of particular events on history and politics.

This kind of work is consistent with Tharp and Gallimore's notion (1988) that learners need a concrete experience they can carry forward to their transaction with a text and then use the experience to create a response that constitutes the learning of something new (e.g. considerations of how the meaning of historical events, including current ones, are shaped and used).

TIMELINES

Timelines help students to build background and context for reading by providing a template. This template helps them during their reading to identify key details, to summarize, to see patterns of textual details, to read along indices, and to discover complex implied relationships and what these mean to the implied textual

A timeline for a story plot. When students make book timelines or historical timelines, it helps them to locate themselves in a text and to visualize and connect various details and meanings.

meaning. Clearly, timelines do powerful work for readers, assisting them in using very sophisticated strategies that many readers never master.

So when beginning inquiry units about historical topics like the Holocaust or the Civil Rights movement, I ask my students to create historical timelines as a way of frontloading their reading. Because they often have no background knowledge on these topics, I might also invite in guest speakers, or we might watch a documentary film.

For instance, to begin our civil rights unit, we watch documentaries, like *Eyes on the Prize*, or movies, like *Selma, Lord, Selma*. These experiences provide foundational background, analogous to the Civil War field trip I just described. Without such experiences, students' learning and reading are not as purposeful.

After establishing some personal connections with the Civil Rights movement, I provide students with lists of important concepts and events from the history of civil rights in the United States. Our readings focus on the African-American struggle for civil rights, and my students work in pairs to research two assigned issues. I then give them a class period to examine with other students in the class how the various issues overlap and relate to each other. The next day, they create a class timeline by putting their items in order on a roll of butcher paper and decorating it with appropriate visuals.

Feel free to adapt the following timeline guide for your own use.

Timeline Assignment Sheet

AFRICAN AMERICANS AND THE STRUGGLE FOR CIVIL RIGHTS

You will be assigned a partner and asked to learn about two or three of the important events or movements listed below. You will then work with everyone else in the class to create a comprehensive timeline of the African-American struggle for civil rights.

You and your partner must do the following:

◆ Identify your chosen/assigned events. (Items that are not chosen in our lottery will be assigned.)

◆ Identify the dates or periods of the given event or movement.

◆ Identify the importance (central focus) and consequences of the cited event or movement. Use the Internet, picture books, articles, videotapes, interviews, and any other resource at your disposal.

◆ Complete a timeline entry, including a summary of the requested information with the name of the event, dates, importance, consequences, and anything else you think is essential for the rest of the class to know. This information will be put on a notecard or printed hypercard sheet, so it can be pasted onto our timeline.

- Complete an artistic or graphic representation to complement your event entry, such as a symbol, picture, photograph, graph, diagram, or chart. You may use the Internet to download appropriate images, but be sure they specifically fit your timeline entry. Be prepared to justify the visual you decide to use by explaining how it exemplifies something essential about your entry.

- Finally, you will put your entries together with those of your classmates to create a chronologically correct timeline. Each pair will read through all the entries on the timeline and create three important connections between entries which will be highlighted through cross-links, call-outs, or labels to help anyone reading the timeline to see the important relationships and themes between events and ideas.

Events and movements that must be included in our class timeline:

- Dred Scott decision (Scott v. Sandford)
- Abolitionist movement/ William Lloyd Garrison and sons
- John Brown at Harper's Ferry
- Lincoln's election
- Phyllis Wheatley (please read Lasky's picture book *A Voice of Her Own*)
- Nat Turner's slave revolt
- Civil War (The War Between the States)
- Battle of Antietam/Emancipation Proclamation
- The *Autobiography of Malcolm X/* Black nationalist movement
- Sit-in movement (e.g., Greensboro, NC lunch counter campaign)
- Chicago Democratic Convention, 1968

- First black regiment in Union Army, 1862 (cf., the movie or book *Glory*)
- Adoption of The Bill of Rights
- Ben Franklin's formal abolition proposal, 1790
- First slaves brought to America
- Plessy v. Ferguson/separate-but-equal legislation
- March on Washington/"I Have a Dream" speech
- Martin Luther King, Jr., life and assassination
- The black power salute at the Olympics
- Race riots in Newark and Watts
- 24th Amendment
- Jim Crow Laws/segregation

- ◆ Declaration of Independence
- ◆ Constitution of the United States
- ◆ Slave importation ban
- ◆ Brown v. Board of Education
- ◆ Assassination of Lincoln
- ◆ Underground Railroad
- ◆ Rodney King trial
- ◆ Breaking the color barrier in major professional sports

- ◆ Publication of *Uncle Tom's Cabin*
- ◆ Selma Freedom March/Freedom Riders
- ◆ Rosa Parks/Montgomery Bus Boycott
- ◆ Assassination of Malcolm X
- ◆ Extra Credit: any other issue, personality, or movement that you find out about that should be on this timeline

Timeline Follow-up Activity

With your partner, please demonstrate your understanding of one of the following questions or issues and your opinions regarding it. Use the timeline as your information source for answering and justifying your response to the chosen question. You may present your response in a radio interview, a play, a video newscast, a collage, a piece of artwork, a newspaper, a hypermedia stack, or another format you choose.

- ◆ What five events, institutions, individuals, groups, or forces were— or are—the biggest obstacles to achieving civil rights and why is this so?

- ◆ What were the most important steps to achieving success in the pursuit of acquiring or preserving civil rights?

- ◆ Who were the most influential reformers in the arena of civil rights and why do you think so?

- ◆ To what degree have we achieved civil rights in this country and across the world? What still needs to be done to both increase and preserve civil rights? Why do you hold these opinions?

SINGLE-TEXT TIMELINE.

Timelines can also be created and used throughout the reading of a single text to placehold what has been experienced and learned. A completed timeline helps students to trace patterns and to see complex implied relationships that occur throughout the text. Teacher Patti Baldwin, for example, has her students create a map timeline of the Oregon Trail as they read Francis Parkman's book on the topic, or a timeline of the events that occur along the Mississippi River as they read Mark Twain's *Adventures of Huckleberry Finn*. Students post significant events in the appropriate places on the timeline and add pictures of these events and descriptions of their meaning. Patti then asks them to go back and visually depict the connections between the events. For example, students can show how Tom and Huck's upbringing informs their treatment of Jim and can help them predict what might have happened in sections of the journey that are not described in the book.

CHARACTER/IDEA TIMELINE.

Timelines can also be used to tell the personal histories of characters, authors, historical figures, or even ideas and movements. Various characters can be displayed on the same timeline to show how their lives differed or were parallel in certain ways. I recently created a character timeline that showed events in the lives of Thomas Jefferson and John Adams. It clearly displayed how the lives and concerns of these two men intersected at times and were removed from each other at others. My class could have easily added Benjamin Franklin, James Madison, and other major figures to this character timeline, since these figures were engaged with many of the same issues surrounding the Revolutionary War and the founding of our country.

BRAINSTORMING

The easiest and most common form of frontloading is simple brainstorming. It is another technique that helps students to move from accessing available life images to creating and internalizing image-making capacities. Brainstorming is frequently used to introduce units because it is an effective way of stimulating, sharing, and recording the class's combined background knowledge about a topic. And scaffolding results when the class shares and records the vocabulary they know, associated ideas, related questions, and their own personal stories. Different methods of brainstorming include the following:

POPCORN/LISTING.

This is a simple activity: just ask students to voice ideas that come to mind—to spout them out like popping popcorn. Have one student list the ideas on the board. The idea is not for students to self-edit but to call out any and every idea.

K-W-L.

A popular way of organizing brainstorming is K-W-L (Ogle, 1983). First, have students list what they *know* (K). Since the group knows more than any individual, all group members are scaffolded to increased understanding. (Also, if someone "knows" something that is in fact incorrect, that misconception is likely to be corrected as all students will be alerted to pay attention to this as they read.) Then ask students to write a list of questions about the topic to which they *want* to know the answers (W). Purposes for reading are therefore set and shared by the group. Students are alerted to the interests and needs of others and are more likely to share answers or interesting information. As students read and *learn*, have them list what they are learning in a final column (L). If they have developed a strong interest and/or have a desire to create a social action project, such as a documentary of what they have learned—they will list information they did not initially ask about as it comes up.

FLOORSTORMING.

For this activity, create various visual displays of images related to the text or unit that is going to be studied. The displays could be any of the following:

- A simple montage portraying elements, ideas, or characters

- A picture map (see page 168)

- A tableau (see page 145)

- The start of a timeline

- A family tree showing relationships or ideas

- Objects and artifacts that will be studied, or that will be important to the upcoming study

- Any other visual that requires students to make inferences, guess at relationships, and pool knowledge about items related to the future topic

Place the display on the floor (hence the name) for a small group to work with. (For a bigger class, the different displays you create for groups to use can be similar or quite different.) Prompt the groups to respond to the displays in specific ways; give directions that focus attention on the images and encourage students to brainstorm from them. For example, before my class read the Inuit folktale "The Fast Runner," I provided a montage of an igloo, a broken spear, a kayak, two men fighting, a sealskin coat, a caribou, a man clothed only in a loincloth, a map of Alaska with two distant points highlighted, a summer village, three men chasing another man who is unclothed, and a judge's gavel. I then provided the following prompts:

- *Look* carefully at the images.

- *Describe* what you see and what you know about these kinds of places and people. *Look* at the relationships between the characters, and between the characters and the setting based on their placements and attitudes towards each other.

- *Infer* what their relationships might be.

- *Look* at the whole display, and note what specific details have in common with each other.

- *Consider* what the topic of the text we will read might be.

- *Share* what you know about this topic.

- *Tell* your group what you know and are thinking.

- *Draw* in or add other details that you know about the topic, places, and people that you think will help you read the story.

Students' responses to floorstorming displays will be scaffolded by the images, which stimulate and support their contributions. Have them record their responses by adding pictures to the displays or by assigning a scribe to record responses in writing.

WEBBING FROM A PICTURE OR OBJECT.

As with any of these activities, adaptations and variations abound. For example, when floorstorming, you might ask each student in a group to choose the picture they know the most about and to draw a web of associations around that picture. Students could then help each other to add to each web.

WHEELS/CLUSTERS.

In this activity, give groups of students different subtopics of a theme to brainstorm, then combine the results into a class cluster or wheel of knowledge. For example, when my daughter's fourth-grade teacher began a unit on the environment, she had groups brainstorm aspects of the environment that affect the quality of human life. She asked small groups to brainstorm everything they could think of regarding how a selected topic— oceans, forests, air, soil, food sources, animal life, geography, climate—might affect how we live, behave, eat, think, and work. Each group made a

Fiona's self/text/world triptych for Alden Carter's *Bull Catcher* helped her access various resources before and while she read.

montage, picture map, collage, or other visual display showing their background knowledge about their topic. The class then created a brainstorming wheel or cluster summarizing their combined background knowledge by putting together all the groups' visualizations. Before combining their finished products, students could walk around to visit other groups' representations and ask questions, make suggestions, and add information.

SELF/TEXT/WORLD TRIPTYCH.

This triptych activity reinforces the essential insight that to read successfully, we must connect our personal knowledge to the text (self–text connections), bring world knowledge to the text (world–text connections), and bring knowledge from other texts and reading to bear (text–text connections) and vice versa. As good readers learn, they connect their reading back to the world, the self, and other texts. To make self/text/world triptychs, students divide a poster board into three equal panels. Prompt them to visualize a topic or an issue related to the reading that comes from their own personal experience. Ask them to create a drawing, collage, or other visualization to illustrate this experience and glue it to the first panel. For the second panel, ask students to draw on their knowledge of history or current events to illustrate connections between the text's topic and the world. This step helps students to identify the larger context for comprehending the text as well as a relevant purpose for doing so. And for the third panel, ask students to create a collage including what they have learned from other, similar texts they are familiar with that might be of use to them. This activity can also be used after a reading to demonstrate what has been learned from a text about oneself, the world, and reading particular kinds of texts.

USING OBJECTS, ARTIFACTS, PHOTOGRAPHS, SCRAPBOOKS

The more interesting, intense, and concrete the experiences accessed or built through frontloading, the better for the reader. For this reason, using objects and photographs related to a text (particularly if they are provocatively issue-oriented) helps students to build up background knowledge, images, and interests for use while reading. Teacher Mandie Victor uses this idea in a variety of ways:

PHOTO GALLERIES.

Before reading texts about D-day with her middle schoolers, Mandie sets up electronic photo galleries on her students' computers (all seventh graders in Maine currently have laptops due to the Maine Laptop Initiative). These galleries contain photos of D-Day preparations, the voyage across the channel, the beachhead, the parachuting, French families, and more. Mandie asks her students to view the photos and make inferences. She prompts them with questions such as: When were these photos taken? Who are the people in the photos? What is the situation? What different groups of people are involved? What are the goals of each group? As they do this activity, students practice the important strategy of inferring from visual cues and also help each other build background knowledge.

VIDEO CLIPS.

Rather than using a whole documentary, Mandie uses short video clips to create interest and build background about a text. For instance, before her D-day unit, her students watch short clips from a PBS documentary about the invasion. She prompts them to ask what the clips have in common and what progression or relationship there might be between clips. As they watch particular scenes, she also asks students to imagine themselves in the role of a combat soldier, an American soldier at a desk job, a dead soldier, a family member from home, a commanding general, a French citizen, or a German soldier. She then asks students to provide an in-role commentary or reflection about the scene from their character's perspective. Students share their responses to learn about the various perspectives involved in this conflict.

SCRAPBOOKS.

To build background knowledge and a basis for later responses, Mandie often creates scrapbooks of important background information with her students before pursuing a unit topic, such as Living Through the Depression. The scrapbooks can be created on paper or simply used in electronic format. Parents, grandparents, community members from a retirement home near school can all help with this project. Students then take over this process, adding to the scrapbooks as they read, or creating one on their own about a character, issue, or theme. In fact, all good frontloading activities should serve students throughout a reading, whether implicitly as a source of information that guides them or explicitly as a template, such as a scrapbook they add to throughout a reading to visibly show the knowledge they are accruing and constructing.

CAMERA CREW.

To show connections between lived experience and text, teacher Brooke Merow sends middle school students out as digital camera crews on scavenger hunts as units are introduced. She might assign them to find a photo that represents an idea or issue, such as something that represents friendship, inequality, or power relationships. Or she might ask them to take a photo that captures a strategic convention—irony, symbolism, humor, a strong mood or attitude—or even a meaning-making device, such as a repeating shape, different kinds of lines, an interruption, or something colorful. Brooke uses these photos as a way to introduce kids to ideas or techniques in the text they are about to read. Kids discuss how certain devices, like color in a photograph, can draw attention to an object or idea. This leads to a discussion of the ways in which authors draw attention to certain objects or ideas. The concrete experience of taking photographs helps students to see connections between their environment and the text, and to use their own photographs as a way of extending their existing thinking in order to understand more sophisticated and abstract uses of these ideas.

VIDEO CLUBS/ART CLUBS/PHOTO CLUBS.

I often run clubs during lunch, a free period, or even after school. These kinds of clubs take little work; you only have to provide a TV and VCR or DVD as well as appropriate media about the topic being studied. Or you can provide art or photo books from the era or about the issue. Just by flipping through books about and magazines from a particular era, kids pick up lots of information and images that motivate their reading. For example, during a study of the Great Depression, I made available several short videos about life at that time, books of WPA photographs, old *Life* magazines, and Cynthia Rylant's book *Something Permanent*, which pairs her original poems with WPA photographs. Some kids were inspired to write their own poems to photographs, others to read more fully about photographer Dorothea Lange. They often made connections between our reading and the visual images I exposed them to.

TEXT-PICTURE MATCHING.

There are a variety of ways to have students match texts and visuals to support the initial phases of comprehension. One way is to provide them with visuals before reading, discuss them, and then ask students to match these visuals to scenes or ideas as they read. The visuals might be photos, picture books, videos, and so on. A variation on this is to have students transform, critique, adapt, or add to the provided illustrations in a text. These basic text-picture matching activities can be extended beyond the frontloading phase and done during reading. For example, you might have students seek out or create illustrations in response to their reading, or ask them to write based on an image from the text. All of these methods assist students in seeing the connection between the words and constructions that make up text and the visual meanings these should prompt in the reader's mind. Great models of the results of these techniques are provided in Douglas Florian's poetry books *Laugheteria*, *Mammal* and *Insects*.

STUDYING ADS AND TEXT STRUCTURES.

To use advertisements in teaching argument and other text structures, gather various advertisements from popular magazines and ask students to look at the shape of the visual details and text, and of the patterns and shapes that are created through objects and layout design. Ask them to identify different structures, such as *compare-contrast*, *definition*, *classification*, and *ironic monologue*. Then have them search through magazines to find other examples of these text structures. Study them together, and ask students how different purposes are served through different structures, how we can notice particular structures, and what the structures ask us to do as readers. (For more on text structures, see chapter 5.) Ask students to identify the following elements of an ad:

- **The claim:** What is the reader being asked to believe or do? Buy this product, or believe this public service announcement.

- **The data/evidence:** What makes you say so? These are specific details that answer the questions (i.e. make this claim).

- **The warrants:** How do you know that the data supports the claim? Warrants explain evidence. (This is typically implied as advertisements are almost always unwarranted assertions that do not explain how the evidence is connected to the claim.)

- **The backing:** How do you know whether the warrant can be believed? (Backing is rarely provided in ads.)

- **Reservations:** Why should you hesitate or question? Why might the claim not be true? (Reservations are also rarely provided in ads, but the reader should certainly actively articulate these.)

- By studying ads together, your class can identify the elements of argument that are present or missing. I often have middle-school students bring in ads and complain that they show unwarranted assertions!

READING PICTURES.

A variety of techniques can help students to study paintings, drawings, photographs, and other artwork to make analogies between what they are doing as viewers or "picture readers" and what they must do as readers of written text. This is a great way of frontloading readers with knowledge of concepts, since you can match the content of the artwork to that of a text. It can also frontload readers with knowledge of procedures, since artists and authors use analogous techniques for communicating meaning, such as comparison, mood, and irony.

I use the art teacher and librarian in my school to access works of art. I show these various works of art on the computer or slides and then ask students to do any of the following:

- **List everything you see in the picture.** I ask them: What was your eye drawn to first? How did the artist draw your attention to this? What are the primary and secondary details? How do they work together? With all of these questions, it is important to connect looking at the artwork to the more complex and abstract issue of

Students study how artists use various techniques to communicate character, movement, mood or an idea.

reading print. For example, point out and explore how authors draw our attention to certain cues they expect us to notice and make meaning of, and that authors link details into patterns to create meaning.

◆ **Identify what shapes and patterns are expressed in the picture.**
   I ask students: How are the details arranged in patterns? Pictures, just like texts, have underlying structures. If we know what the structure is, we can know better how to read the image or the text. Explore how to see patterns in a text by paying attention to transition words, how to see compare and contrast details, and how to see cause and effect.

◆ **Find the detail that is most salient or powerful to you.** I ask: What in the painter's technique or in your experience made this detail stand out? Point out that authors also use various techniques to make words or phrases stand out. (A great text to use to teach this kind of highlighting is *Someplace Special*, a picture book about civil rights illustrated by Jerry Pinckney.)

◆ **Study this picture and the relationship between objects and/or people.** I ask: What's the story? What has already happened? What will happen? What is the relationship between the objects, ideas, people? What is the feeling or emotional content of the relationship? (Renoir's "La Loge" or Munch's "The Scream" are great for helping students to infer answers to these questions.) Discuss how authors also leave gaps for readers to fill in.

◆ **Compare the relationship in the picture to a relationship in their reading.** I might compare Mary Cassatt's "Mother Sewing" to the relationship of the uncle and nephew in the picture book *Uncle Jed's Barber Shop*, or to that of Hester and Pearl in *The Scarlet Letter*. Then I ask students: How do the artist and author display facts and feelings about the relationship? What do we learn from this about what we must attend to?

- **Look at certain pictures and examine a specific feature or technique.** I ask: What different techniques were used? What effects did each technique have on you? Different authors use different styles and techniques to communicate various elements, such as mood or character. Ask students to jot down all the physical descriptions of a character provided by an author and to consider how they highlight particular details, or to consider whether they use any kind of repetition to reveal character attributes.

- **Look at different works by the same artist, or treatments of the same theme by different artists.** I ask: What is similar or different? What differing meanings are communicated through different treatments?

UNDERSTANDING PERSPECTIVE.

To teach the power of perspective and point of view, art teacher Marilyne Schottenfeld reads a passage from *Stuart Little* as students follow along. From Chapter 8, she reads aloud about Stuart's mother (a human being) mistakenly shutting Stuart (a mouse) in the refrigerator. 30 minutes later she finds him there, struggling to keep warm on the butter plate. Marilyne then asks students to create two illustrations to show what Stuart saw when Mrs. Little opened up the refrigerator door and what Mrs. Little saw when she looked inside the refrigerator. She has students fold their drawing paper in half and lightly sketch their ideas with pencil. Marilyne prompts them to consider the expression each character would have at the moment they see each other.

A student sketch of what Stuart's mother sees when she opens the refrigerator door.

Students draw over their sketches with black pens, then share and discuss them in groups, comparing what details from their lives and from the text helped them create their pictures. Marilyne has found that this kind of work, before or near the beginning of a reading, ". . . gets kids not only to the ballpark, but actually into the game. Once they've made the first couple of plays, they need much less help to keep going."

MARRYING POETRY WITH ABSTRACT ART.

Marilyne likes to invite her students to study how abstract art conveys meaning. After discussing a few works of art together, she asks them to select a favorite poem. They then choose a medium that they think would best convey the mood and ideas of the poem. Marilyne asks them to incorporate some actual lines from the poem into the art. They may do this by writing directly on their artwork, or they may choose to glue lines from copies on to their artwork. Or they can use other art supplies to blend the words into their composition, so they look like they belong to the abstract piece.

Students share and explain how their artwork captures their vision of what the text means.

A natural follow up is to have students find a piece of art and then to write a description of it, a commentary, or a poem that "paints the picture in words" or captures the feeling and emotion of the art. Marilyne finds this a great way to frontload kids through writer's block—"They can't say they don't have anything to write about, and our discussions of art and writing have shown them what things they need to notice and how to make meaning of these cues."

CLASSIFYING CONCRETE OBJECTS/PICTURES.

Teacher Gerrie Netko begins many of her elementary units with a classification game in which she asks students to sort pictures or objects about the upcoming unit into different groups. I observed her introducing a unit on the characteristics of life with just such an activity. She provided students with photographs of various organisms and objects, such as rocks, amoebas, animals, stuffed animals, and fossils of extinct creatures like trilobites and dinosaurs. She first asked students to place each picture into the categories "living" or "nonliving." They quickly realized that to refine the sorting process, they needed additional categories, such as "extinct."

After discussing the life characteristics implied by each class of photos and individual examples, Gerrie asked students to define what makes something animate or inanimate, and then pushed them to begin to define characteristics of life by looking for shared traits and by comparing the pictures they had classified as living to those in the other groups. On the heels of this, she asked students to do a **"sketch to stretch"** activity. She read a short essay entitled "What is Life?" and asked students to draw images of what they saw in their minds as she read. When done, she asked small groups to create a picture that would summarize the overall point of the essay about what constituted life and what was not living.

Gerrie told me that most students captured only one main idea from the text and did not represent the concept of a life span as a sequence of birth, growth, maturity, maintenance, aging, and death as described in the essay. This gave her valuable information as she planned how to teach the unit on cell biology and the biology of organisms that followed this frontloading activity.

Such an activity can lead to work on writing extended definitions, a very important type of writing in scientific classification. This kind of writing is also the basis for most laws and legal interpretations, and is important in ethics, medicine, and math. (See chapter 5 for more on reading and writing extended definitions.)

RESOURCES

Below are some books to give students as models for illustrating poems and songs.

Double Vision by Michael and Peter Benton which matches masterworks of art with poems written about them

Something Permanent by Cynthia Rylant which matches WPA photos to Rylant's original poems

Talking to the Sun by Kenneth Koch and Kate Farrell is a compendium of poems and collages

I, too, Sing America: Three Centuries of African American Poetry by Catherine Clinton, with illustrated poems

Love to Langston by Tony Medina, a poetic picture biography

Cool Melons Turn to Frogs: The Life and Times of Issa by Matthew Gollub, which juxtaposes biography poems and illustrations in an interesting manner.

Hoofbeats, Claws and Rippled Fins, edited by Lee Bennett Hopkins

Creature Poems by Lee Bennett Hopkins

Earth Always Endures by Neil Philip, which matches photos to poetry by Native Americans

Knock at a Star; A Children's Introduction to Poetry by X.J. and Dorothy Kennedy

This Land is Your Land by Woody Guthrie. Artist Karen Jakobsen uses oil landscapes of iconic American images to amplify the story of this musical composition

GRAB BAGS.

Elementary-school teacher Phyllis Bull uses a technique she calls "grab bag" to provide students with the visuals they need to approach a story. She puts photos, found objects, maps, and other visual connections to a text in a bag, and gives one bag to each student as a resource to "take on your reading journey!" After reading, students are asked to create their own grab bags. Phyllis's directions for students to create their own grab bags are as follows:

- Identify story facts, such as the major characters, settings, and conflicts, as well as personal ideas and responses such as the issues, concerns, "ah-has," and themes that you discover as you read.

- Collect objects, pictures, and drawings that represent ideas from the text that are most important for you to remember. (Students may choose to focus on text facts, on ideas and responses, or both, depending on their needs and classroom purposes.)

- Label each item in the bag to explain its connection to your reading of the text.

- Put the title, author, and a picture representation of the text topic and main idea or theme of the text on the bag. Decorate the bag to illustrate these ideas.

- Try to have at least six items in your grab bag. Share your bag with your literature circle group. Be prepared to explain what your objects mean to you as a reader of the text.

Phyllis provided me with this example of how one might create a grab bag: "For my reading of *Roll of Thunder, Hear My Cry*, I might decide that the book is about the fight for equality. So I might choose a photo of a potholed dirt road to help me symbolize the feeling of the children as they walked to school and were splashed by the whites-only school bus. I might make a picture of a school bus with a broken axle. This "victory" over the school bus represents their fight to be equal. I might also put in a picture of a Cadillac to show how Uncle Hammer tried to show he was as good as the white people, of a weightlifter to show how Mr. Morrison used physical strength to protect his rights, of a brain to show how Papa used strategy and smarts to help preserve their rights. I could put in a piece of cotton and a match to show how Papa saved TJ from being lynched. Maybe a picture of a white lawyer to show how Mr. Jamison tried to help. Or a simple piece of red paper to signify the anger they all had to overcome, if they were to survive."

"ARTWORKING" ONE'S WAY TO UNDERSTANDING

So many times I have witnessed students laughing and sharing as they study pictures or talk about their drawings together. I have seen students who were clearly resistant and unenthusiastic about beginning a new unit working excitedly to infer the similarities among several pictures. They could figure out through the pictures what our unit theme was and often discovered that they could connect the unit to prior knowledge and interests.

I remember Jamaal, at the end of an inquiry unit on the question "Who were the greatest figures in the Civil War?" telling me: "Hey, the drawing was absolutely key, you know? If I hadn't done those drawings at the start, and made the scarves for the different characters, and talked about it, I wouldn't have understood the big conflicts and issues . . . what was at stake. . . . Then it was easier to read the stuff and to talk about it and to see what was important about learning all this and how I was connected to it. I could see how we are all still connected to it, politically and all. I kind of drew and 'artworked' my way into being able to understand."

Jamaal is right on. All of these frontloading activities invoke Vygotsky's notion of "thought on the way inwards"—students acting, drawing, talking, and visualizing their way from concrete images and hands-on visual strategies to more abstract meanings and complex comprehension processes. That's why frontloading is so key—it helps us achieve our ultimate goals!

CHAPTER 5

Time *After* Time

Sequencing Strategies That Help Students Meet the Next Reading Challenge

*A*s we explored in the previous chapter, frontloading is the first instructional move a teacher makes toward improving students' comprehension. It opens the gate for students to achieve a deeper understanding of content, to develop new interests, and to use new reading strategies. This chapter explores how to follow frontloading with instructional sequences that further develop students' reading and thinking abilities.

Good teaching is like good parenting.

The sequences of support may include readings, visualization activities, and other rituals that scaffold students' abilities to higher and higher levels. Later in this chapter, I share some great activities to carry this out, but first I want to place these sequencing strategies in a teaching-learning model that is crucial for you to buy into! When you embark on using any of the visualization strategies, this model will give you the "pegs" to hang them on for sustained, successful instruction.

SEQUENCING IS LIKE GOOD PARENTING

My biggest teacher research project ever has been raising my daughters. How my wife and I taught them to read is a good first example of instructional sequencing. We gave our daughters cloth books about the same time they first gummed infant cereal, and we were astounded at how quickly babies can understand concepts of print—turning pages, looking at pictures, anticipating the funny parts, and so on. In time, we involved our girls in many activities that might seem tangential to learning to read, like going to the zoo, planting a garden, and talking about movies. These experiences gave them language they could use later in speaking and then reading.

We knew that our daughters would not learn to read in a day, a week, or even a year. We were in for the long haul, establishing a sequence of life and reading experiences that would help them to grow memory by memory and text by text. We knew we would need to keep introducing them to more sophisticated texts when they had the ability, interest, and need for them. We also knew that we had to allow ourselves and them ample time to make reading happen.

My wife and I carried around books and modeled our own reading passions. We read aloud constantly, sometimes acting out scenes. As our daughters grew up, we kept upping the ante. Children's picture books were replaced by juvenile picture books, graphic novels, then young adult books and magazines, such as *Sports Illustrated for Kids*. When the girls displayed interest in a specific idea or issue, a certain book, author or particular kind of text, we provided them with ways to pursue these interests. When appropriate, we provided slightly more challenging texts that built on their existing interests and abilities. I read these texts aloud to them, talking about my reading. Sometimes I even left adult versions of the text-type about the house. This kind of availability is important: Children can't advance unless we make available the next accessible challenge.

My wife and I have done much of this intuitively, in some ways almost haphazardly, as many parents do. We didn't sit at the kitchen table and map out an instructional plan for teaching our kids to read from ages three to ten! But as a teacher, I have come to articulate how this same teaching-learning process between parents and children can—and should—occur in schools. The process I embrace is much like putting the pieces of a giant puzzle together. Students learn to become strong, independent readers when teachers help them add new reading strategies piece by connecting piece. Gradually, a coherent picture emerges, revealing the complete set of mastered skills possessed by proficient readers.

SEQUENCING IN A NUTSHELL

Sequencing is all that you do to teach and support students through a significant zone of proximal development. It is modeling at the point of need and providing whatever support is necessary to complete significant tasks. We sequence instruction to make sure that we are continually raising the bar for students, moving learning from the concrete to the abstract and fostering significant new strategic abilities.

SEQUENCING TAKES TIME

As simple as it might first seem, assembling a puzzle isn't a speedy endeavor. It requires patience and perseverance, just as both teaching reading and learning to read do. The process calls to mind one of my favorite sayings: "Eat your elephant one bite at a time." One step at a time is the only way we can successfully address big challenges.

Sequences are sustained endeavors because all deep learning occurs through repetition over time, as we gradually layer new meanings on top of established ones. For example, in vocabulary instruction (Brown, Collins, and Du Guid, 1989) research shows that the average teenager has learned 17 words a day throughout his life simply by using language. In contrast, studying lists of words and using them in sentences, as we often do in schools, does not build vocabulary. With this kind of studying, definitions are rarely learned in a meaningful way and are quickly forgotten. For example, in learning the word "cap," a child might first imagine, based on experience, that it means a black woolen hat for the head. Through hearing "cap" repeatedly, the child learns that the word can refer to various kinds of tight-fitting headgear (skullcaps, baseball caps, and so on) as well as to other objects that cover the top of something, such as a polar ice cap. Eventually, the child learns that "cap" can also be a verb that means to top off something, as in "capping spending." Achieving a deep and flexible understanding of any word takes time and requires repeated experience of the word in meaningful contexts.

This kind of naturally occurring "sequence" is sometimes referred to as "tacit instruction." Some researchers (Hillocks et al 1971; Beach and Appleman, 1984) argue that repeatedly reading a text convention or structure in a kind of informal sequence can help us to know how to read, interpret, and use these conventions. But other research (see, for example, Smith, 1987) shows that explicit sequences of instruction in how to use different text tools and conventions (such as ways to recognize and understand symbols, irony, or inference gaps) lead to more efficient and powerful learning, particularly for students who may not read widely or who struggle with reading. This kind of sequencing work is known as "apprenticing" readers into expert practice.

In any event, some kind of sequence is necessary for us to deeply understand the demands of a particular text—the demands of its vocabulary, ideas, and text conventions—and thus apply appropriate strategies to comprehend it. Taking the time to guide your students through sequences leads to the profound, transferable-to-life learning that rarely occurs in schools because of our headlong push for coverage of information.

> ## CHILDREN AT WORK
>
> **R**esearchers have shown (Collins, Brown and Newman, 1992; Hillocks and Smith, 1988) that sequencing helps children to gain deep knowledge of content and the strategic tools that can be used to understand concepts in new situations. But teaching sequentially takes time, as all good teaching does. The payoff is that good sequences lead to deep learning of foundational concepts and strategies that will be used throughout a student's life.

SEQUENCING IS BASED ON AN APPRENTICESHIP MODEL

The major idea behind sequencing is that we must apprentice students (Collins, Brown, Newman, 1992) to become more expert at such cognitive skills as those that make up reading. The apprenticeship model is built upon four key elements that are essential to deep learning:

- The **social context** of the students and of the learning. All people learn best in real situations!

- The treatment of **content,** by teacher and student, as a tool—a form of social action that can accomplish things in the real world

- The **method** of the teacher, who focuses on assisting student strategy-use and gradually releases responsibility for that strategy-use to the student

- The **sequencing** of activities and materials from the known to the development of new strategic capacities

Situate It

In all learning-centered models the sociology of the learning is key. Learning should build from students' interests and abilities and connect to their current social context. Learning should be purposeful and problem-centered because learners need the opportunity to observe, invent, practice, and hone expert strategies in a context of real use. They also need to get feedback within the context in which knowledge is developed and used.

These authentic situations are filled with sensory details that assist learning, and many of these details are visual. For example, the best way for me to learn how to cross-country ski is by skiing down a trail with a teacher. Within that context, I receive feedback from my performance and from my teacher, and use this to adjust my technique. I can quickly discover whether my herringbone technique is good enough to make it up a hill. If it's not, my teacher can offer tips, model techniques and I can immediately see if and how certain adjustments work. The context of use is therefore essential to my learning this particular skill. If I only talked about cross-country skiing techniques, or only tried them in my socks on the living room floor, I wouldn't learn to ski. You might laugh at the exaggeration of this example, yet this type of learning, which is divorced from real contexts, is all too typical of what frequently happens in school.

Offer Multiple Contexts

The cognitive research base shows that using skills in multiple contexts during a sequence greatly assists students. In learning to ski, I'd want to try different trails, with hills and different pitches and turns, in order to gradually make things harder. If I can adapt and transfer my technique to different situations, then I have truly learned it. The same is true of reading: Trying out different inferencing skills by using cartoons, photographs, fables, and short stories greatly increases inferencing ability.

Model It

Students also benefit from seeing various models of expertise in use. They need to experience masters (teachers and other experts) and apprentices (other students) engaged in meeting target skills at varying levels of expertise. This provides benchmarks of progress and helps them to identify their own strengths and weaknesses, goals for improvement, and alternative ways of solving the strategic problem at hand. Visuals are excellent for showing and sharing how different students use particular strategies.

Make It Social

Authentic situations are intrinsically motivating. Students tend to improve their skills when they are participating with others—when there is a social reward for advancing their skills. For example, when I could first ski up a hill, and later when I completed my first ski marathon, the thrill at my growing competence was exquisite, and it was enhanced by the applause of my skiing buddies.

Children thrive when they are given a chance to collaborate.

THE CONTENT: A MEANS TO AN END, NOT AN END IN ITSELF!

Curricular content is typically regarded as established sets of information (the WHAT), usually packaged in textbooks. This became painfully clear to me when I went to our local school's parent night. Several teachers talked about quizzes, standards, state tests, and the importance of "getting the required information." No one talked about learning how to be a better reader or problem solver, or about achieving deep mathematical or historical understanding.

In cognitive apprenticeship, the emphasis is placed on learning strategies that help us do something (the HOW). The WHAT is still important; but there is recognition of the fact that we learn content most deeply by using it to think, problem solve, or argue—by using it to actually accomplish something. Strategies and the content they operate on, and the relationships between them that are created when we solve problems, can all be powerfully taught and modeled through various visualization techniques (as illustrated later in this chapter).

MAKING INFORMATION USEFUL

Learning-centered teachers believe that "content knowledge" includes the following strategic procedures that make information usable and powerful:

Heuristic strategies: rules of thumb and other intellectual tools that guide problem solving

Control strategies: comprehension monitoring, evaluating, decision making, and applying knowledge to real situations

Learning strategies: strategies to use in finding, acquiring, and integrating new information into our schema

Text-specific/genre strategies: comprehension strategies required by particular kinds of texts (arguments, satires, classifications, ironic monologues, lyric poetry)

Task-specific strategies: comprehension strategies required by a particular convention or text-code that can occur in any kind of text. e.g. readers must detect cues for symbolism, irony, foreshadowing, inference gaps, and then construct implied meaning.

SEQUENCING GUIDES STUDENTS TO INDEPENDENCE GRADUALLY

Visualization techniques can be powerfully used at each phase of instruction.

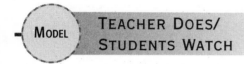

MODEL | TEACHER DOES/ STUDENTS WATCH

The expert (usually the teacher) carries out the task in a real situation so students can observe the process; visual models of the completed task, in which the use and "social work" of doing the task is highlighted, may also be provided.

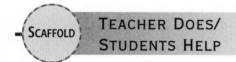

SCAFFOLD | TEACHER DOES/ STUDENTS HELP

The teacher carries out pieces of the task that students cannot yet manage and asks students to help in ways that they can manage. The teacher provides assistance and prompts.

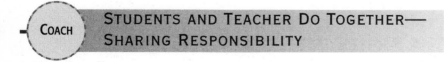

COACH | STUDENTS AND TEACHER DO TOGETHER— SHARING RESPONSIBILITY

As students gradually assume more responsibility, the teacher helps by prompting and assisting—articulating the knowledge, reasoning, and problem-solving processes of the expert; naming the processes and ideas students are using; and naming or modeling what students are not yet doing but could do next. The teacher names and demonstrates what kids need to do.

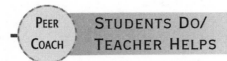

Peer Coach | **STUDENTS DO/ TEACHER HELPS**

Students work together. The teacher helps only if and when needed, coaching through feedback, hints, reminders, prompts, and scaffolding.

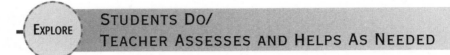

Explore | **STUDENTS DO/ TEACHER ASSESSES AND HELPS AS NEEDED**

The teacher fades into the background, encouraging student autonomy in problem-setting and problem-solving. Students independently meet tasks as the teacher assesses and plans future instruction. Students are allowed to set their own questions, frame problems, and pursue their own reading and inquiry.

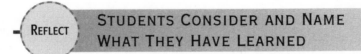

Reflect | **STUDENTS CONSIDER AND NAME WHAT THEY HAVE LEARNED**

Students are assisted with consolidating their learning by comparing their own problem-solving processes with those of experts and other students. Students are helped to set goals for future learning.

In many ways, the learning-centered approach leads to student-centered learning, as kids use what they have learned to pursue their own agendas and do their own work—the goal, I would argue, of all learning.

SEQUENCING TAKES STUDENTS FROM THE KNOWN TO THE NEW

When you select texts and activities for an instructional sequence, the following principles will help you plan:

Your texts and activities should move from:

◆ the visual and visually supported to the less visual and visually supported;

- the "close to home" (near to student experience) to the "far from home"—from the most accessible to the least accessible; from the students' current abilities to the gaining of new abilities;

- the direct and literal to the indirect, with high inference loads;

- the concrete to the abstract;

- the short to the long;

- the global to the local, and then back again to the global (students begin with an understanding of global purposes— they know why they are learning the strategy and how they will use it immediately and in the future);

- teacher-involved to student-involved;

- similar tasks to more diverse forms of the task;

- performing the task with similar texts to performing it with a variety of texts;

- from collaboration to individual.

THEORETICAL LINKS

These principles for planning sequencing activities are consistent with schema theory and transactional theories of reading. They are all based on the understanding that learning proceeds from the known to the new, and must be grounded in students' current experiences, interests, and abilities.

SEQUENCES ACCOMMODATE ALL LEARNERS

Sequences can accommodate individual differences in interest and achievement, differentiating instructional support across various groups or individuals. This can happen when all students are involved in learning the same strategies for similar purposes, or when they are inquiring into different aspects of the same topic or inquiry theme. For example, different students can be variously:

- **Working on the same strategy through different texts that are appropriate to their interest and abilities.** Some students might work on inferencing with picture books, while others hone their inferencing strategies through short stories or young adult novels.

- **Working on the same conceptual topic but through different texts or text-types.** Some readers may be reading picture books about race relations, like Polacco's *Pink and Say*, as others read young adult nonfiction, like *Now Is Your Time*, popular magazine articles, and newspaper clippings about the same topic. And more advanced readers may be reading even longer and more sophisticated treatments, such as *Coming of Age in Mississippi*.

- **Working with various levels of support.** The teacher can work with some students (TEACHER DOES/STUDENTS HELP) while other students work together (STUDENTS DO TOGETHER/TEACHER HELPS) as the teacher comes around occasionally to prompt them. Or students might use exit tickets to help shape the next day's work, while others could be in the final phase of the sequence continuum, working through texts in small groups or on their own (STUDENTS DO/TEACHER WATCHES).

In each of the above cases, all students are involved in the common inquiry projects of the class and benefit from each other's work through sharing and reflection. With the current legislated emphasis on assisting all students, and on raising achievement between minority groups and special education populations, such sequencing structures adequately challenge and appropriately support learning for *all* students in the classroom. Inquiry-based sequences can therefore help you to teach for each student's strongest self and to promote their potential in the most powerful ways, while still teaching a unified unit to the class.

Sequences for Finding Main Ideas

I n this next section, I'll demonstrate how to bring all these
pedagogical ideas to bear on some useful sequences for
teaching reading. Strategies like making simple inferences as
well as seeing complex implied relationships across texts are
both necessary to comprehending main ideas and the themes
of complete texts.

DISCOVERING THEME OR MAIN IDEA: CONNECTING THE AUTHOR'S DOTS

One of my favorite sequences is designed to teach students how to find main ideas, which is obviously important to the reading of any kind of text in any subject area. To discern main ideas, readers must first identify the topic (the general subject of a text), then they must identify the key details. But these two steps are not enough. Expert reading requires readers to understand the relationships between details, and through this understanding to comprehend the main ideas about the topic. The main idea or theme is an idea that goes beyond the text—an idea that can be applied to the world.

Main ideas can be directly stated, which typically happens in informational text and arguments. They can also be simply implied by the patterns of key details, which is usually the case with literature. For readers, the challenge—and the joy—is to connect the dots of these patterns in order to discern what the author is saying about life. For example, to understand what Lois Lowry is saying about the topic of protecting civil rights in *Number the Stars*, we must look at the pattern of what the Danes—and in particular the Johannssens—did to protect their Jewish neighbors during World War II. We must then look at what the Jewish population did to help themselves. And finally, we must consider which actions worked and which did not. Only seeing across the patterns of these details can we understand the point Lowry makes about the topic of protecting civil rights (e.g. that we must work together as an entire community to define and protect these rights).

Identifying main ideas and supporting these with evidence from the text are skills that our national assessments (the NAEPs) continually show only a minority of our graduating seniors actually possess. And the numbers for these higher level skills are decreasing, perhaps as a result of our renewed emphasis on teaching information instead of strategies. On the last NAEPs, published for 12th grade, only six percent of high school seniors were found to possess these proficiencies—a shocking finding. How can students become active citizens of a democracy if they cannot discern and judge the central underlying principles behind texts, such as speeches, proposals, and op-ed pieces?

READING FOR MAIN IDEAS: A SAMPLE SEQUENCE

The type of main idea sequence described here can be used—and, as the statistics suggest, is certainly needed—by all students to improve their skills in identifying and providing evidence of main ideas. With various adaptations, it has been successful with students of all abilities, from elementary school through high school. Here's how it played out in a unit on adolescent health I did recently with middle schoolers. As I plan the unit, I consider two elements that I must deal with from the outset:

◆ **I set the social context.** I first introduce the inquiry question: What is healthy living? The class and I then brainstormed subquestions, such as: What do we need to be healthy? What are the biggest health issues facing tweens and teens? I tell students that we will interview several healthcare professionals, do a lot of nonfiction reading, and eventually engage in small-group research about topics that have come up that are of great interest to them. At the end of their small-group inquiry, they will create a multimedia proposal about improving the health conditions of our school or community.

◆ **I introduce the content.** Through activities and readings, I introduce students to several content topics around our inquiry question, such as nutrition, drugs, exercise, independence and parental relationships, social acceptance, and dealing with pressures. Each activity or reading is issue-oriented, including how additives and certain kinds of food preparation can harm our health, how the misuse or even the sanctioned use of drugs can change body functions and threaten health, how life habits such as video gaming can encourage physical indolence, and other issues of mental and physical health appropriate to the group, since my initial strategic goal is to help the students identify various subtopics of our inquiry theme.

I DO/YOU WATCH

After sharing the inquiry question, I open the unit by providing them with a collage of different kinds of junk food. I reveal one picture at a time and I talk my way through what I see as the similarities and differences between each new picture and the succeeding ones. In this way, I can think aloud about how topics are discerned through the common elements between key details. A topic, in fact, is what all the key details hold in common, and it should be expressed as specifically as possible.

I next show students a collage of individual athletes involved in basketball, soccer, tennis, golf, swimming, and running. I ask them to list each key detail— there's a boy playing soccer, a girl hitting a tennis ball, and so on. Finally, I ask them what the topic of the collage is, reminding them that this would be the general subject of the collage. To find this, we need to find the most specific category we can that would include the common elements of each of the key details, since a topic is what every key detail has in common.

I focus on key details. My students typically identify the topic as "sports." When I ask them why it couldn't be "games," they argue that sports and games differ in certain respects. For example, they might suggest that games are played more for fun than for winning, or that they don't require sweating and aerobic activity. I usually can agree with their ideas, but then challenge them to come up with a more specific topic statement. If they don't come up with "competitive sports," I offer it myself.

Some students might disagree with this topic statement because all of the pictures are of individuals. So how can we know that these people are competing with someone else? Together, we examine the details of the pictures—lane lines in the pool, dress jerseys worn by the basketball player and runner, the lights shining on the soccer player—which lead us to infer that every individual pictured is indeed in a competitive situation. Some students might then offer that the topic is "individual performance in competitive sports," since each photo is of an individual and this is a key shared feature. I tell myself and my students, "Now we are getting somewhere!" And I also ask them what the first collage has to do with the second one, so they can see the connections between the different topics that we will study (junk food and exercise are both aspects of adolescent health, our inquiry topic).

I follow with a similar activity. This concept of "classing" or grouping common elements is a pre-requisite to reading, writing, and understanding classification and extended definition text-structures. So I reinforce the last activity with the Five Guesses Game, for which I give my students a list, revealing the items one at a time: potato chips, Mudpies, nachos, twinkies, donuts. As each item is revealed, I guess what the topic might be. I make various mistakes and ask the students to correct me. They must explain first how they know I have made a mistake, and then how they know their topic statement is better.

YOU DO/I WATCH

After I have modeled the game, I ask students to play it on their own, and I provide help as it is needed. I reveal the list one word at a time. Students write down a guess as to the topic of the list each time a new item is revealed. With each new item, they can revise or confirm their previous guess and explain why. To up the ante, I put one item in the list that doesn't fit; in this instance, that might be a healthy snack in the list of junk food. This requires them not only to identify and explain the topic but also to identify the oddball item (apples) and the basis on which the item does not fit the topic expressed by the other five examples. (In this case, answers could include any of the following: an apple is a healthy food; it is a natural instead of processed product; it is a complex carbohydrate instead of a refined one; it contains natural fructose and does not contain refined sugar or fat.)

The stated object of the game is to guess the topic as soon as possible, but the real object is to understand how the commonality of key details expresses a topic and what makes a group of key details members of an identifiable class.

Next, I get to the central focus, or main idea. Once students have identified the key details and the common topic they share, I can ask them what statement the details seem to make about this topic. I return to the collages and ask them to identify the comment that is made by the connections or pattern across each of the pictures. I tell them that this statement will be the central focus, or its main idea.

In the case of the sports collage, students typically come up with ideas about the importance of effort to athletic endeavor, or how athletes develop the ability to focus and expend effort (all of the photo subjects have facial expressions that show intense concentration and focused effort). In the case of the junk food collage, students typically come up with notions about how good junk food looks, but how bad such foods are for you, as each of the pictures presents the junk foods in very attractive ways. This part of the process helps students to understand how key details work together to express the central focus, or deep meaning of the text.

I recap the process we've been through. Throughout the sequence, each time I introduce a new idea, I coach students in what to do and give them some practice. Then I begin to gradually release responsibility to them, allowing them to coach each other (YOU DO TOGETHER/I HELP). At the end of the sequence, we articulate the heuristic, or problem-solving script we followed to identify topics and key details, to see the relationships and patterns among the details, and to infer the point made by these relationships. At this point, we can reflect on how to apply this script in our future reading. When you try this idea with your students, don't hesitate to actually state the learning benefit, and the terms. Tell them that the ability to see the connection among details and how these connections or patterns create meaning is called inferencing, and it is essential to good reading.

IDENTIFYING THE MAIN IDEA IN VISUAL TEXTS

After running through introductory sequenced activities such as those described above, my students generally have the terminology and strategies necessary to identify topics, key details, patterns across key details, and implied central focus statements—at least with collages and lists. Then it's time to add something to the sequence, so I make things harder by adding a different, more difficult kind of text, as you'll see below.

Now that students have the basic script down, I start this next sequence of more difficult activities at the YOU DO TOGETHER/I HELP phase. I can always move back to I DO/YOU HELP with students who exhibit difficulties. Likewise, as soon as some students show they have met the new challenge, I allow them to move on to independent practice. In this way, I learn from the students what to emphasize, and my teaching is always responsive to their needs, so I can give small-group or individual attention as needed.

PAINTINGS AND PARODIES.

I often center a more challenging sequencing activity on famous paintings and parodies of these paintings, since parodies change salient details to shift the topic and, therefore, the central focus of a painting. This shows kids how changing even one key detail can radically alter the topic (which must accommodate all key details) and the central focus (the statement about the topic which must consider all the key details). And it demonstrates how attentive a good reader must be.

For example, when I introduce Grant Wood's famous painting "American Gothic", students usually identify the topic of this artwork as "farm life." Occasionally, they think the topic is "married life." I constantly ask students to justify their topic choices, which requires them to justify their thinking in a way most high school seniors cannot do with text. We practice with these visuals and then move to the more implicit meanings in written texts. So to support the topic of farming, my students might cite the farm house, the side of the barn, the pitchfork the man is holding, and the plain workclothes worn by both the man and the woman. To support the topic of marriage, they cite that the picture shows a man and woman standing together in front of a house. The two are placed close to each other in front of a home we can assume they share. The plain churchlike window of the house's second story implies a religious basis for their enterprises. Their expressions are stolid, careworn, and tired, which my students associate with marriage!

Either of these topics works because both can be justified with details from the text. Realizing this conveys to students that different readers might identify different topics for the same text. This means that it's fine for readers to ascribe different central foci to this same artwork even when they're paying close attention to all of the same codes in the text. Interestingly, the central focus statement is similar for either topic here: "Marriage is tough" or "Farming is a hard go." The evidence is the same for both: the tired and haggard looks of the couple and the plain worn clothing.

I then show students Richard Hess's parody of "American Gothic", in which he simply adds gas masks to the face of the man and the woman. My students get a good laugh, and then I ask them how we must revise our notion of the topic

American Gothic by Grant Wood   Richard Hess's parody of *American Gothic*

based on this new key detail. Prior to the 9/11 terrorist attacks, most of my students identified the new topic as "pollution," though some who lived in farm communities identified the topic as "toxic fertilizers." Post-9/11, my students almost always identify the topic as "bioterrorism." This clearly shows the transactional nature of meaning making: Based on the knowledge and concerns readers bring to bear, a text will address a different topic and make a different point to them. This new point accommodates the codes of the text and the readers' knowledge base, questions, and current needs or interests.

The key details now also include the farm, but the gas masks are more important. The central focus students usually identify is something along the lines of "Air pollution is everywhere, even out in the country" or "None of us is safe from bioterrorism, even those who live in the country." Both farm life and an airborne threat are essential to establishing the central focus statement as this statement must account for the gas masks.

PRACTICE WITH MORE DIFFICULT TEXTS

After you try activities like the one above, which uses pictures, practice the process of identifying a central focus with increasingly difficult texts. First, try using texts with less visual support, then move to texts that are longer and more abstract, and finally to texts with topics further from students' background experience. To start this process of increasing the difficulty, I use combinations of visuals and text—photos with captions, or comics and political cartoons—so that students must look for patterns across the visual and written text. Then I move to short texts like picture books, illustrated poems, non-illustrated poems, and short stories or articles, practicing the same techniques and using the same terminology. I pay attention to the students and how much practice they need. I don't move on to more difficult texts until they understand how to use the process with simpler, concrete, and more visual texts because the concrete experience with visual texts scaffolds their abilities to the point where they can use the same strategies with written texts.

FINDING THE CENTRAL FOCUS IN POEMS.

After a couple of days, my students and I are reading poems, such as Shel Silverstein's "My Rules," which starts with "If you want to marry me, here's what you'll have to do . . ." I ask students the topic of the poem. The title and first line give strong clues that the topic is "Rules for marrying somebody." We then identify the key details of the poem, which are mostly the rules themselves: "darn my socks," "be still when I talk," "shovel the walk when it is snowing." Some students think it is also key to infer the gender of the speaker, which is not identified. Most kids think the demanding tone sounds like a male, but some think that since males traditionally ask females to marry them, that the speaker must be a female. If the students identify the speaker's gender as being a key detail, then I remind them that this must be reflected in the central focus statement.

The poem lists many rules that must be followed, and concludes with the final line: "Hey! Where are you going?" The poem's details lead to this central focus: "If you set too many rules and demands for marriage, the person you love will leave you." Or, if a student felt the gender was crucial, the central focus might be: "Men should be careful of setting too many rules for their wives, if they want them to be happy." When students can independently apply this process without the support of visuals, a measure of independence has been achieved—the

Engaging kids in sequences of collages, cartoons, and short texts can cover a lot of ground in a very little time, giving kids lots of practice with finding main ideas. It also allows you to turn your teaching around on a dime. For example, if I am using a collage that I discover is too conceptually difficult for my kids, I have wasted just three minutes and can get the lesson back on track immediately. But if I try to teach the same processes while teaching a novel, I might waste four weeks before realizing it didn't work. Shorter is better. Repeated use of a strategy with different texts leads to expertise.

sequence has begun to do its work.

WRITING SUMMARIES AND OTHER EXTENSIONS.

Make no mistake: Reading for the central focus, or main idea, is a profound achievement, a key part of a foundational educational competence. And reading for the main idea must be honed with each new kind of text a student learns to read. Whenever you successfully complete a sequence with students, they are ready for a new one. For example, students who can read for a main idea can easily be helped to compose excellent summaries. Writing summaries can be contextualized and applied through various activities, like writing telegrams, creating picture-book summaries, or creating a set of prompts that encourage a complete summary of a particular text-type.

One More Time!
The Benefits of Repeated Readings

A very impressive research base demonstrates how students of all ages benefit from rereading. In fact, the work of Sulzby (1985) and others in the field of emergent literacy demonstrates that children learn how to read by rereading. Anyone with small children knows this is true: They drive you crazy rereading the same book hundreds of times! Rereading is a form of sequencing, as each reading provides background and competence with which to approach the next reading. Because the child understands the basic meanings, her intellectual resources can then be used to attend to new words, more sophisticated text features, meanings, and more.

Interestingly, in the American schools where I have worked, teachers are often adamantly set against allowing students to read books they have read before. The only explanation I can find is that they believe that teaching is purely purveying information, so if students are familiar with the *information* in or plot of a text, there is no purpose for rereading it. But if we are dedicated to assisting students with developing transferable *strategies* of reading, thinking, and problem-solving, then rereading is an essential tool of our teaching. It allows students to develop competence with strategies. This practice of rereading is used extensively in the German, Swiss, and English schools where I have worked. Teachers in those schools seem to understand that deep comprehension and strategic knowledge are developed through this process.

REREADING A POEM WITH VISUALS: A SAMPLE SEQUENCE.

I recently saw teacher and former Oregon State Reading Association President Peter Thacker use prereading and rereading in a session he conducted at the West Regional IRA meeting. Peter chose a poem that was about one page long and full of images. In fact, any text that is image-rich will work, including a fable or very short story.

Peter started with the strategy of visual prompting. He read the piece aloud, asking us to keep our eyes shut and to "watch the TV screen of our minds" to identify major images. We did not have copies of the poem, so we had to listen carefully. Peter then reread the poem, this time asking us to try to more fully capture the most important images, adding details and specificity to them. On a third rereading, we were told to more fully imagine and flesh out the details of the strongest images. Notice that each reading served as a prereading (or frontloading) for subsequent readings, and by the end we had done a deep study of the poem by focusing on creating visuals.

For the next reading, Peter asked that we draw the strongest image we captured from the poem, adding the words that fed the image on our drawings. The final step involved Peter reading the poem aloud yet again, stopping at any point anyone indicated that he had created an image. That person presented their image to the class at this point, explained why he found the image to be so strong, and then posted it on the wall. As each succeeding image was presented, it was placed in sequence on the wall from left to right. Interestingly, several participants drew images from the same textual prompts, so there were clusters of images at two points in the poem. These images were placed vertically along the timeline of images we created. When we were done, Peter asked us if any strong images had been left out. He then asked for volunteers to create drawings to fill in these spaces.

As a class, we then did a gallery walk of our images to notice visual themes—images, colors, tones, shapes, implied actions, or ideas that seemed to recur. We also noticed how different people envisioned the same prompts in different ways and explored why this might have happened. Some images were iconic, some abstract, others very true to life; these different images captured different readers' experiences. At this point we were well into discussing the visual images, the poem, and what we were learning from this activity.

We had been supported in seeing the poem, identifying key details, ordering these details, seeing patterns across the details, and inferring the meanings of these patterns. Then we were asked to justify the discerned main ideas with details from the text. Peter helped us turn the poem into a collage that made the poem more accessible, and on which we could operate interpretively, just like the collages I described in my main idea sequences.

The activity was a powerful sequence in itself, but it could also serve as a kind of frontloading for subsequent readings of other poems or texts using similar concepts or requiring similar strategies.

READING BETWEEN AND BEYOND THE LINES WITH VISUALS: A SAMPLE SEQUENCE.

Art teacher Marilyne Schottenfeld has developed an excellent short sequence that helps students to see the difference between reading as literal decoding and reading as seeing stated or simple implied relationships (reading line-by-line, bringing accumulated meanings forward); reading as seeing patterns of more complex implied relationships (reading between the lines, filling in implied and missing meanings); and reading as elaboration and connection to concerns outside the text (reading beyond the lines to make text-to-text, text-to-self, and text-to-world connections). Her sequence helps students to develop strategies for reading in these different ways. Expert readers make use of all these kinds of reading simultaneously as they read almost any text. This sequence therefore helps Marilyne's novice readers to get a fuller view of reading expertise in a visually supported way.

It can be used with any text of short or moderate length; she likes to use it

The Owl and the Pussy-Cat

with the poem "The Owl and the Pussy-cat" by Edward Lear.

The Owl and the Pussy-cat went to the sea
  In a beautiful pea-green boat,
They took some honey, and plenty of money,
  Wrapped in a five-pound note.
The Owl looked up to the stars above,
  And sang to a small guitar,
"O lovely Pussy! O Pussy, my love,
    What a beautiful Pussy you are,
      You are,
      You are!
What a beautiful Pussy you are!"

Pussy said to the Owl, "You elegant fowl!"
  How charmingly sweet you sing!
O let us be married! Too long we have tarried:
  But what shall we do for a ring?"
They sailed away, for a year and a day,
  To the land where the Bong-tree grows
And there in a wood a Piggy-wig stood
  With a ring at the end of his nose,
     His nose,
     His nose,
  With a ring at the end of his nose.

"Dear Pig, are you willing to sell for one shilling
  Your ring?" Said the Piggy, "I will."
So they took it away, and were married next day
  By the turkey who lives on the hill.
They dined on mince, and slices of quince,
  Which they ate with a runcible spoon;
And hand in hand, on the edge of the sand,
  They danced by the light of the moon,
     The moon,
     The moon,
They danced by the light of the moon.

by Edward Lear

READING/DRAWING LINE BY LINE.

Marilyne's goals are to use the sequence to help students create initial visualizations and to build metacognitive awareness—to know how they form mental representations as they read. More than that, though, she wants them to become aware of how mental pictures change and build upon each other as the poem's lines unfold and more information is provided. Literary theorists call this "reading along indices." It is the expert strategy of carrying meaning forward through a reading, of constantly accruing and revising meaning as one gains new information and encounters new cues.

The ice skating rink inside the city gates of Old Quebec, the subject of Jasmine's poem.

Marilyne puts the poem on the overhead and covers up all but the first line of the first stanza. She has her students fold a piece of large white drawing paper into eight boxes. In the first box, she asks them to draw a small pencil sketch that captures the mental picture they create based on information from the first line. She then uncovers the second line and asks students to repeat the procedure. She does this for each line for the first eight lines of the poem. (They do not draw the three-line refrain.)

When finished, each student analyzes their progression of line drawings to see how each line provided new visual information to add. Students share their renderings and consider how mental pictures differed and developed as new information was provided. They then create a final illustration that combines all or some of the line-by-line pictures into an image that best represents the meaning of the whole stanza. Finally, Marilyne allows students to

---

QUEBEC

When we go to Quebec
We go up and we go down.

We go up the steep ramp
to go down the ice toboggan.

We go down the funicular
to visit La Petite Quartier.
We go up the funicular
to go ice skating.

We ski up the hills.
We ski down the hills fast!

We walk under the city gate
to go down town.
We look up to see the
beautiful white city lights.

We walk up and down the city streets.
We stop to eat delicious crepes.

We sled down the hills
to the St. Lawrence Seaway.
We walk slowly back up
the hills to the Plains of Abraham.

When we go home,
we dream of
up and down
in Quebec.

add color and other pictorial elements, and to share and reflect on similarities and differences.

READING/DRAWING BETWEEN THE LINES.

Marilyne then proceeds to the next activity, which is designed to help students gain awareness of how good readers read between the lines by creating suggested subtextual meanings, bringing their own personal experience into conversation with the text. This is done in order to fill in gaps or extend and complete patterns left by the text.

She asks students to reread "The Owl and the Pussy-Cat" and to create an illustration that goes with the explicit text but fleshes out and adds "unmentioned" details to stated meanings. Her prompts might include:

- ◆ What kind of boat do you think they took out to sea? Draw an illustration of the pea-green boat as you picture it. Why did you add the details that you did?
- ◆ What do you think a "bong tree" is? Draw an illustration of how you see it and explain why you see it that way.
- ◆ What are "mince" and "slices of quince", and what is a "runcible spoon"? Draw an illustration of this place setting at the wedding banquet, including eating utensils and food.
- ◆ Draw a scene from the wedding reception and celebration.
- ◆ Come up with any other complete picture that is suggested by the text but is not provided or provided fully.

Students complete their visual renderings and compare them with each other. They consider differences in how they read between the lines and discuss how life experiences, knowledge levels, and text details might account for these differences.

DRAWING/READING BEYOND THE LINES.

The final activity in this sequence is designed to show how readers go beyond the text to elaborate meanings, infer future events or associations, and connect what has been read to new and quite different real-world situations. These processes allow readers to achieve some form of transfer, as they use textual experience to think about events or issues outside the text.

To start creating a new set of textual meanings, Marilyne tells her students that they will create a rendering that explores probabilities and possibilities not discussed in the poem. These should build on the text to continue the story or apply the textual meanings to new situations. Her prompts might include:

- The owl and the pussycat are, of course, two different species. Draw a picture showing their future offspring.
- Owls and pussycats prefer different kinds of abodes. Design a dwelling that would satisfy the needs and desires of both.
- Predict what their future life will be like and draw a scene from that life. What in the poem and in your experience informs this prediction?
- What particular joys and obstacles do you predict for their union? Draw a two-sided tableaux that pictures one joy and one obstacle in their life together.
- What kinds of other unlikely relationships and alliances (familial, political, and so on) do you think this poem might also apply to? Create a collage of unlikely relationships or make a flow chart about how such a relationship might begin and develop.

This sequence leads students to see details, connect these details to make

Video Club

Video clubs can be used in a sequence to build conceptual knowledge about a unit theme. I have students arrange to meet in self-chosen groups over a weekend and watch a video from among several choices.

For example, for an inquiry unit on "What is success?" students could choose to watch *Finding Forrester*, *Forrest Gump*, *La Bamba*, *Good Will Hunting*, and *Clockers*. Younger students might choose *Pocahontas*, *Shrek*, *Aladdin* or other movies that explore various notions of success.

Check out the reference *Videohounds Golden Movie Retriever* for summaries of movies that are classified around curricular themes!

On the next page is a response sheet you can adapt for use with your students.

Note: This sheet can be adapted for use with any inquiry theme.

VIDEO CLUB RESPONSE SHEET

After you have watched the movie together, answer the following questions as a group. Feel free to talk with your parents and other adults as you do so.

TITLE OF MOVIE(S) YOUR GROUP WATCHED:

1 Describe how success is portrayed in your movie, i.e., what messages about the image of success and achieving success are communicated?

2 Is the image of success conveyed by the movie you watched similar or different from the image of success you hold and/or that our society holds?

3 How do the images of success in this movie compare to other cultural images of success such as those in other movies, in songs you know, and on television?

4 Is there something we need to do about the cultural image of success in our society? If so, what can we do about it? How can we overcome or change the cultural image of success in our own lives?

FOR EXTRA CREDIT:

5 Visit some Internet sites that feature visual images of success, such as humanityquest.com, home.cogeco.ca/~rayser3/literal.htm, or other sites.

6 Find and read poems about success, like "Success" by Edgar Guest, "Still I Rise" by Maya Angelou, "The Road Not Taken" by Robert Frost, "Richard Cory" by E.A. Robinson, or other poems.

7 Coment on what is being communicated about success through the web images or poems.

various kinds of inferences, and to think about the text as connected to the larger world. Obviously, it helps them to think about the deep thematic meaning of the poem as well.

THE RIGHT TEACHING TOOLS

Frontloading and sequencing are the big levers in my teaching tool belt. They pry kids from where they are and get them moving to where they might go next. One year I taught Kris and Stephan, two struggling and reluctant readers. They complained vociferously about our new civil rights unit until, during the frontloading activities, they realized that sports involved profound civil rights issues and that they would be able to read about this.

Through their readings about the Negro Leagues, about Jackie Robinson and Hank Aaron, I led Kris and Stephan through sequences that helped them to understand new perspectives, to see patterns and connections, and to make inferences. For example, later in the unit, when they balked at reading Dr. Martin Luther King, Jr.'s "Free at Last" speech and "Letter from the Birmingham Jail," I told them that they already knew everything they needed to read these texts. To Kris's dumbfounded "Huh?!" I explained that they could use their knowledge of black ballplayers' experiences and their own work on taking new perspectives to understand Dr. King's situation and writing. And, with a little more assistance to both boys, I was right. They each drew a picture of both settings—the mall in front of the Lincoln Memorial and the Birmingham jail cell—along with pictures of what King hoped to transform through the words he spoke and wrote in these places. The boys created picture maps of each text with topic, details, and central focus. More than that, they used these artifacts to discuss the connections between breaking the color barrier in baseball and Dr. King's struggle, and then compared the two King texts in insightful ways.

Stephan complained with a smile that I had tricked them: "You taught us what you wanted us to be able to do by letting us read what we wanted to read." I had to admit that he was right because the "trick" he described is exactly how we move kids along the trajectory of their potential.

CHAPTER 6

Making *the* Scene!

Seeing and Summarizing Characters, Events, and Situations

When I first began to draft this chapter on summarizing, a student named Bam came to mind. He was part of the boys and literacy study I did with Michael Smith, and an aficionado of the World Wide Wrestling Federation and Extreme Championship Wrestling. Bam kept incredibly detailed journals about the wrestlers' careers. During lunch, he would often entertain his classmates by performing a simulated sportscast of the previous night's matches. His classmates depended on his summaries to keep up with the shows. In addition to watching matches on television, Bam read trade magazines about

Ask yourself: Do you know your students well enough to teach them.

wrestling like Mick, another boy in the study who pretended he was the wrestling character Captain Jack. Bam often play-acted roles from wrestling shows. He took bets on Smackdown, (a round of staged championship wrestling bouts) based on the plot conventions that helped him predict what kinds of things would happen. Once, when asked if the wrestling was real, he responded, "No way, man, these are soap operas for guys!"

One might say that Bam was doing everything an English teacher would want: he was totally engaged with the stories, he could placehold facts and relate them to others, he cared about characters and entered into their experience—even to the extent of pretending to be a character. And he wrote to keep track of what he had seen, and to analyze the shows so that he could make predictions and see hidden meanings. Considering all of this, Bam should have been a fantastic English student. Instead, he was failing. When asked why, he launched into a passionate monologue that went something like this: "I won't learn from that woman . . . she doesn't know me, she doesn't care about me, she thinks I'm a blank slate to write on, an empty cup she can fill up with her stuff. She doesn't know that I bring things to the table, and she doesn't care to know that. So I won't learn from her."

Other students of mine made similar comments:

> "[School] is not about us. We aren't even in the equation."
>
> "The teachers don't care about us or our stuff. Why should we care about them or their stuff?"
>
> "I want to do something that shows who I am. The teachers never let me do that. I am always doing *their* work instead of *my* work. So nobody [in the class] can get to know me, I can't show who I am or who I want to be. School is just a waste of time to me and I don't think the teachers are ever going to change."

Comments such as these are unnerving. They prompt me to consider: Do I know my students well enough to teach them? Do I privilege and use what they bring to the table? Do they know I care about them?

Bam and his peers wanted to be recognized and to make a human connection to their teachers. They wanted to connect personally with the content of the curriculum and to do work that identified themselves as vital, evolving people. These students reminded me that in order to teach well, I must harness the social power of the classroom. This chapter explores how I have tried to do this in using a cluster of visualization techniques around the skills of summarizing and inferring. These strategies allow students to reveal who they are and who they want to be as they interact with characters, settings, and situations in personally meaningful ways.

These strategies help students to:

- notice, identify, and envision key details about characters, situations, and events;

- combine details to create a complete story world or mental model;

- use visualized details to create summaries;

- connect and synthesize details to make various kinds of inferences;

- use visual details as tools to think with, construct, and interpret implied textual meanings.

The Skill at Hand
Inferencing

First, let me define inferencing, the skill all techniques in this chapter ultimately lead to. Inferencing is an essential element of all sophisticated reading tasks, particularly tasks where we read to learn or understand something new. It involves the ability to see connections, relationships, and patterns between various details and parts of a single text. But readers also need to make inferences between texts and beyond texts. These relationships of connections might be between the world and the text, between one's personal experience and the text, or between similar texts or texts about the same topic.

George Hillocks (1980) cites several kinds of relationships between text details that the accomplished reader must discern and understand in order to make inferences.

Authors often use a "directly stated relationship" between two or more ideas. This is literally presented information and does not require making an inference. Nonetheless, readers must identify and remember the connection, which is typically causal. More sophisticated and challenging are what Hillocks calls "simple implied relationships." In these, the separate details are close to each other in the text and provide different pieces of information about a similar idea or theme. It is up to the reader to discover the nature of the relationship between the pieces of information.

"Complex implied relationships" occur when a reader must connect a large number and variety of different details spread across different parts of the text (or across different texts in an in-depth inquiry, such as understanding history, legal precedents, or different points of view). To make such inferences, students must be able to "identify the necessary details, discern whatever patterns exist among them, and then draw the appropriate inference from the nature of the pattern" (Hillocks, 1980, 308). This is something that fewer than six percent of American high school seniors can do, and it is essential to creating knowledge and new understandings while reading (cf. NAEP, 2003).

"Authorial generalizations" (a central-focus statement for a text) must be inferred unless an author directly states his or her main point (which rarely happens, particularly in literary texts). This requires students to infer and articulate the main point a text implies about a particular topic. Students must consider "the proposition(s) that the story might be said to represent" (Hillocks, 1980, p. 308).

Finally, there are "structural generalizations", an explanation of how a text is constructed to make a particular point and how the various parts of a text work together to make that point. "[This] requires the reader to explain how parts of the work operate together to achieve certain effects" (Hillocks, 1980, p. 308). Authors never explain how their texts are structured to emphasize and highlight these effects and ideas, so these insights must always be inferred.

The ability to see connections and infer their meaning is complex and incredibly important set of skills. But inferencing depends on the ability to identify key details and to bring these forward throughout a reading so they can be connected to new key details. In this way, summarizing is a skill upon which all other higher levels of interpretation and thinking depend. To introduce and hone all of these skills with your students, try beginning with an entry point that Bam and his buddies would approve of: delving into character. It's a starting point that builds nicely on the frontloading techniques explored in chapter 4, as these techniques start with the known—an exploration of the student's character—and then connect to the new—to unfamiliar characters, ideas, and authors of texts. Understanding the known and the literal is a prerequisite to understanding the new and the implied.

Understanding Character

Understanding character is essential to comprehending a fictional text. To get any satisfaction from a story or novel, a reader must understand what motivates characters, how they change over time, how they relate to each other, and how their interactions and motivations drive the plot. And readers must also understand where characters stand at a story's end.

Character is also important in historical narrative and informational texts. After all, human history is the story of people's experiences through different times, contexts, and events, and these personal experiences resonate with young readers.

In my studies for *You Gotta BE the Book* (1997) and *Imagining to Learn* (1998), I found that good readers often insert context and character into texts where this element is missing or only implied. For example, when reading a word problem that involves a recipe, a reader might imagine

HELLO, AUTHOR

When students connect with the author and consider the intelligence behind the text, they begin to read in a more engaged and "dialogic" fashion. Encourage them to ask questions during and after reading, such as:

Who wrote this?

Why did she write it?

For whom did she write it?

What is the point of the writing? What kind of thinking or social action is it intended to promote?

Exploring questions such as these is central to critical reading.

himself actually preparing that recipe. When reading an essay in favor of wearing school uniforms, a reader tends to create a sense of the author and actively contend with her.

The benefits of this peopling and personalizing of texts are great. When character—or a pronounced authorial perspective—is made part of informational-text reading, the reader's meaning making is energized by this human dimension. Indeed, I've found that students strive to imagine a human need or function that can be played out with the information they are reading (Smith and Wilhelm, 2002; Wilhelm, 1997; Wilhelm and Edmiston, 1998).

ACTIVITIES THAT HELP STUDENTS TO INFER CHARACTER

This first group of activities helps students to infer character. They also help students to make other kinds of inferences related to characters—about settings, a character's relationships to others, historical periods, situations—and to pay attention to visual details that can be resources during their reading. The beauty of these strategies is that everybody can see, hear, and assist each others' reading and thinking processes, as students work on these projects together and then present them.

Blueprint for Introducing All the Techniques

Below is a series of steps to keep in mind as you use the strategies for summarizing and inferring with your students:

1. Model your use of a visualization strategy with a text excerpt.
2. Have students read the next text passage aloud, silently, in pairs, or in small groups. Encourage them to keep in mind and use what you have modeled.

3. Brainstorm—either as a whole class or in small groups—to list salient images, details, or scenes on the board or chart paper.

4. Discuss how everyone pictures the details, scenes, and characters and why each person envisions the scene as he does.

5. Create a visual artifact (individually or in groups) to capture some aspect of textual meaning.

6. Share and discuss visual artifacts, noticing how they are alike and different; articulating what they express about the text's meaning; and looking to see if there are patterns that show up across the artifacts.

In step six, I often have students post their work and then walk around to view it. Sometimes I ask them to write questions or comments on a clipboard posted next to each artifact. We then use these notes to fuel a class discussion. As a variation, I invite half the class to walk around while the other half sit with their work and discuss it with their "wandering" classmates. After this activity, students can read the rest of the text, alone or in pairs, and try to use the modeled technique.

> ### "GIVE ME THE STORY"
>
> "**M**aybe I would read a person's story about slavery and how they get through. Yeah, that sounds pretty good, but I don't want to read about the whole timeline of slavery…" Geo says it all. Students are drawn to the stories of individuals, not disembodied facts. And research bears this out. Character is highly important to student reading interest and engagement. (Wilhelm, 1997; Smith and Wilhelm, 2002 Wilhelm and Edmiston, 1998)

PERSONALITY PROFILE.

At the beginning of the school year, have students write personality profiles of themselves. You might also pair students to write profiles of each other, which has the benefit of allowing students to get to know each other while they learn to conduct an interview, check facts, and write a compelling profile.

Students can create hypermedia cards or Powerpoint slides about themselves that include scanned or digital photos of themselves involved in favorite activities or in a favorite context. My students sometimes include audio files of favorite songs and video clips of themselves or of friends talking about them. But whether done as a writing assignment or a high-tech presentation, this activity works nicely as an ice-breaker for students—and it's a great way to review the aspects of character that must be understood by a reader, including:

- Physical appearance
- Typical dress
- Favorite activities
- Favorite books, movies, music
- Modes of speech and language used
- Ways of interacting with others
- Personal quotes, ways of talking

- Beliefs and opinions
- Emotions and reactions
- Soapbox topics (strong beliefs)
- Favorite places and typical surroundings
- Friends and other social relationships/groups belonged to
- Responses of significant others
- Quotes from others about them

Students build knowledge about character and characterization as they work together to write personality profiles.

EXTENDING THE HYPERSTACK PROFILE.

The personality profile hyperstack can be shared and built on throughout the year. For example, students can add character cards, author cards, or idea cards. On a character card, a student describes how the character is similar or different in appearance from himself, how the character's beliefs differ or are similar to his own, or how the character experiences relationships in ways similar to the student. To write an author card, a student articulates how an author's attitudes seem similar or different from her own, which requires understanding authorial generalizations. And on an idea card, a student expresses how a text sparked or developed an idea, or how his understanding of an issue was transformed through the reading.

WHAT STUDENTS HAD TO SAY:

Joe, a seventh grader, after plugging characters from *Roll of Thunder, Hear My Cry* (Taylor, 1976) into his personality-profile hyperstack, wrote:

> I learned that I am a lot like Cassie because I get offended when I am treated unfairly. But I learned I am better off than her because my family is not going to get killed if I stand up for myself, which was something that could happen to her back then. And I learned that there are different ways of dealing with problems. Like Papa always made a plan to solve problems through the back door, by being smart and tricky. Mr. Morrison used physical strength, but he was quiet about it. Uncle Hammer used anger and putting it in people's faces. Putting them [these characters] in my hyperstack made me realize I am most like Uncle Hammer, which surprised me, but I think it is smarter to be more like Papa, so I am going to think about how to be more like that.

Katie Hutchison's portrait of Cassie Logan, which she embedded into a hyperstack about her family and how they compare to the Logan family.

The possibilities for building on personality profiles and the benefits of doing so are many. At the end of the year, the students will have a sophisticated hyperstack that shows how they have connected to the various characters, authors, and ideas encountered throughout the year. They will have also deeply explored what makes us human and marks our identity as well as various ways of being in the world. To me, this is one of the major purposes of reading and of a democratic education.

BODY BIOS.

I first learned about body bios at an NCTE conference, and it has become a favorite of my students ever since. In this activity, which is very much a grown-up version of the classic Kindergarten activity, students trace their bodies on long sheets of butcher paper. They then color in the forms using a variety of symbols and labels. There are many methods of filling in the forms; one of which is creating an anatomically-based biography. In this type of body bio, the brain area is used as a place to put images about the subject's interests, personal knowledge, and expertise. The heart area is where emotional attachments, passions, strong opinions, and feelings are symbolically portrayed. At the eyes, favorite books and movies might be portrayed along with a representation of how the individual typically sees the world. At the stomach, favorite foods are shown, and at the mouth, the subject's typical style of language. Arms and legs are used to show favorite activities, and so on. The area of the paper surrounding the figure could be used to visually describe favorite places or typical surroundings. As with the hypermedia project, I like to have students create a biography of themselves and then one of a character or author, which is a more challenging endeavor. They can then use the biographies to forge connections with characters, comparing similarities and differences in backgrounds, concerns, situations, strengths, and weaknesses.

WHAT STUDENTS HAD TO SAY:

After sixth grader Sarah created one of these for herself, and then a parallel one for Annemarie of *Number the Stars* (Lowry, 1992), she wrote:

> [Doing] this kind of slaps you in the face and wakes you up! I never thought much about what a potty mouth I am, and how much junk food I eat. Wow! And this made me think even more when I compared myself to Annemarie, who had no junk food to eat, and who had to be loyal and true to her friends and family or they could all die. Maybe her responsibilities made her that way, that good and that serious. Maybe I don't have enough responsibility? (Don't tell my mom!) It made me think that I am a big softie and I better get it together. If I had to live through what Annemarie did, I don't know if I could do it.

READING IS SEEING

DRESSED-UP BODY BIOS.

Other students I've taught have clothed the figure created in the body bio activity and then surrounded it with symbols and biographical details. Everything they chose resonated with deep meaning about their character. Details might include props, accessories, jewelry, characteristic colors, and quotations from and about the character. Other writing on and around the figure can be used to reveal the character's virtues and vices, concerns, obstacles faced, major ideas, significant others, typical actions and activities, and defining moments.

WHAT STUDENTS HAD TO SAY:

Tanya, a seventh grader, offered a powerful insight about this activity when she told me:

> You know how you are always talking about making our reading and thinking visible so we can test it out? Well, I think the dressed-up body bio is great because it makes us as people visible to each other . . . I like that. It's like I'm finally learning about other people, and with them and from them instead of sitting all alone at a desk.

NAME TAGS.

Teacher Sharon Stein at the Rutgers Writing Project introduced this simple technique to me. On the first day of school, Sharon has students create their own large name tags that represent themselves—their strengths, interests, feelings, and so on—through art. She provides them with a variety of materials to use for decorating their name tags, such as glitter, markers, wrapping paper, and buttons. The twist is that their names cannot appear on the name tag. Students create their name tags without looking at each other's

Jasmine's nametag for Count Olaf from Lemony Snicket's *A Series of Unfortunate Events*. The mask shows that he is a master of disguise, the dollar bill shows his greed, the black car shows his mobility and penchant for showing up "at the wrong place at the right time." The "eye" is his tattoo.

Jasmine's personal name tag, showing her interests in playing basketball, running, softball, reading, playing the clarinet, love of pizza and animals. She has added her name after presenting the tag to the class.

work. When everyone is finished, each student pulls one tag out of a box where they have been placed. In turn, each student shows the class the tag they drew. The class studies the tag, lists the details they see, and draws inferences about the person who created it and what they were trying to communicate. The point is not to guess the name or person who created the name tag, but simply to make inferences about the creator. The student presenting the name tag sums up the inferences made. When the class is done, the student asks who made the name tag and delivers it back to her.

You might also give students the names of different characters or authors the class has read about and ask them to make a name tag for the character or author of their choice. Then have students present the name tags, making inferences to guess who from the unit the name tags symbolized.

SELF-PORTRAITS/PORTFOLIO FOLDERS

Kip Plaisted, a teacher at our national demonstration site for adolescent literacy in Washington County, Maine, has his students create a self-portrait, which they use to adorn their portfolio folder. He then has them decorate their folders in the same manner as the name tags in the above activity. Kip's students also fill out an interest survey that he uses throughout the year to monitor how well he is meeting student interest, and to guide him in suggesting free reading choices and so on. The completed survey is laminated and placed inside the folder. The outside of the folder is therefore a visual expression of each student's personality, and the inside of the folder is a written expression of that students needs and interests. The folder itself will hold the work that the student completes throughout the year, marking his growth and identity.

PICTURE TALK.

One of my favorite techniques for helping students infer character is something I call a picture talk. I simply find photographs of interesting-looking characters. Then I show students a photograph and ask them to make inferences about the character of the person in the photograph based solely on the visual details. One of my best sources for doing this is a photo book of candid portraits taken during the sixties—kids love the photos of hippies, policemen, and students with their bell bottoms. To get them started making inferences about such characters, I might prompt them to:

Imagine these two characters meeting somewhere. Where might they meet? What would they say to each other?

◆ Freewrite: identify anything you see and what you think it might help you know about this person.

◆ Describe the person.

◆ Imagine what she or he is looking at.

◆ Imagine what she or he is thinking. Put it in their own words as a stream of consciousness.

◆ Imagine what this person's job is.

◆ Decide where this person lives. What is this person's favorite hangout?

◆ Describe what this person will eat for dinner.

◆ Imagine what this person's nickname is.

◆ Decide what this person's favorite movie, book, or song might be.

◆ Imagine what this person's soapbox topic (something they care intensely about) might be.

◆ Write a brief monologue about this topic from the person's perspective, using the person's language.

In each case, I ask students to justify their inference. What in the picture, and in their own personal experience, might lead them to their conclusion? We talk about the need to justify inferences, the necessity of keeping initial inferences tentative and open to revision, and how inferences need to be confirmed by various sources of information. We also discuss what we need to observe and know about these characters to have confidence in our inferences.

Then the fun begins: I put two photos together and ask students to make inferences about the relationship between them. The more incongruous or provocative the pairing, the better—put a hippie with a dress-suited conservative looking person, for example. I prompt students to consider:

- Where might these two meet?

- In what situations might they meet?

- What are they thinking when they see each other?

- Who begins the conversation?

- What does she or he say?

- How does the other person respond?

I then ask students to write down their imagined dialogue between the two characters, and they always have a blast with this. They must justify what they have written by naming the visual cues that inspired them. I then explain how we must visualize characters and make these same kinds of inferences based on the textual cues we get during reading. As a variation, I might present photographs of people who look similar to characters in a novel we are reading and link that activity to the book.

PICTURE TALK VARIATION: HISTORIC PHOTOGRAPHS.

During a unit on the Great Depression, my students explored this inquiry question: What happens when the structures in one's life break down? Students tried to understand what it must have been like to have no money, to lose a family house and farm, and to have siblings go far away to find work. We studied and responded to WPA photos of people and asked: Who are these people? What might their names and ages be? Are they related? What are they doing? How are they feeling? What does the head of the household do? What are their plans? What do we foresee for their futures?

We also studied photos of settings without characters, asking: What is this place? Who might live here? Why does the place look as it does? What events have happened here? What might happen? What might be a conflict that might happen here?

In this Great Depression unit, we used two books by Elizabeth Partridge. The first is a biography of Dorothea Lange for young people called *Restless Spirit*, which includes photographs of Lange and reproductions of her famous photos. The other is Partridge's book about Woody Guthrie called *This Land Belongs to You and Me*, which includes his songs, photos, and drawings. We also used the book *Something Permanent* by Cynthia Rylant, which matches her original poetry to classic WPA photos.

A yearbook page for *Charlie Bone and the Time Twister*. Pictures include the time twister, a calendar page for the day Charlie went back to 1916, a magic wand to show his magical powers, a pair of glasses to show his ability to see the future and see through pictures.

PICTURE TALK VARIATION: POSTCARDS.

Postcards, art postcards, or prints of paintings can also be used with the picture-talk technique. Sharon Stein uses art postcards and asks students to do the following:

- Tell a story about a character in the painting.

- Respond as the person in the painting: Why did you pose this way? What were you communicating about yourself and your situation? How happy are you with the painting? Tell us your life story as the person in the painting.

- Create a dialogue with a character from another painting.

GREAT BOOKS THAT USE VISUALS

Prairie Visions: the Life and Times of Solomon Butcher by Pam Conrad features archival photographs taken by pioneer Butcher to punctuate narrative vignettes from pioneers.

Kids at Work: Lewis Hines and the Crusade Against Child Labor by Russell Freedman uses archival photographs by Hines, which he took to document the horrors of child labor. This book is a good example of how visual information can be a form of social action.

Romare Bearden: Collage of Memories by Jan Greenberg and Romare Bearden is a dynamite biography of African-American artist Bearden. It features various Bearden compositions with companion text.

Steamboat: The story of Captain Blanch Leathers by Judith Gilliland is a fascinating picture book biography of the first female River Steamboat captain.

Hottest, Coldest, Highest, Deepest by Steve Jenkins depicts the most extreme places on our planet using collage illustrations.

The Top of the World: Climbing Mount Everest by Steve Jenkins includes stunning photographs of climbers and the Himalayas.

Tuesday by David Weisner uses triptychs of illustrations to show action at different points. It's great for teaching perspective and sequences.

Sundiata by David Weisner offers a brilliant use of composition to get across setting and action.

Sumo Mouse by David Weisner, presented in a comic-booklike format, demonstrates various ways of telling narrative and using motifs. It's great for teaching inferencing based on visual patterns.

MORE ACTIVITIES FOR EXPLORING CHARACTER

YEARBOOK PAGES.

To help students delve into how characters express and portray identity, assign them the task of creating the yearbook pages for various characters. As a senior yearbook page might, these pages must include favorite activities, classes taken, leadership roles, friends, and seminal events. I sometimes then have my students assume the role of the character whose yearbook page they designed and sign each other's pages in that role. Bind all of the pages together into a Book Yearbook.

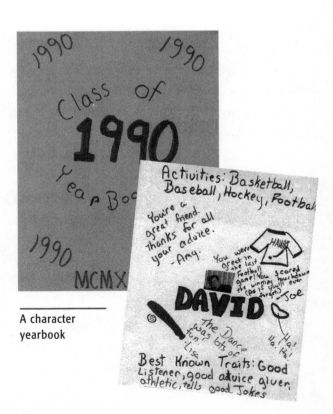

A character yearbook

ILLUSTRATED CHARACTER JOURNALS.

In or out of role, students can create character diaries or journals and illustrate these with drawings, magazine cutouts, clip art, and so on. These can be respectful, but sometimes students cannot resist making them satiric, making their descriptions comic or humorously critical.

Two excerpts from illustrated character journals for historical figures.

CHARACTER INTERESTS/EMOTIONAL DISPLAYS.

In an idea several of my student-teachers have adapted from Phyllis Whitin's excellent book *Sketching Stories, Stretching Minds* (1996), kids can be asked to create a pie graph of their own average day, interests, and emotional make-up and then to create one for a character, so they can compare and discuss what these findings show about personality and values. Students also enjoy adapting this idea to create self and character stress-o-meters (showing how different situations cause different levels of stress, reactions, and so on.), value line graphs (the various degree to which values are embraced or displayed by a character or author) and Chinese nest boxes that display the difference between outward appearance and values and inner ones. These techniques can also be used to explore and display the emphases, focus on various characters, values, emotional content, ideas and themes expressed by a book. Again, these decisions should be justified based on textual evidence.

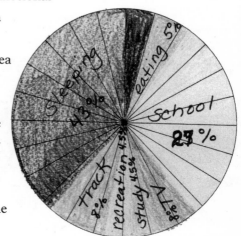

Melinda's pie graph shows how she spends her time on a typical day.

This symbol map shows that Tintin has a sense of adventure (ship), is brave (the sword), loves to travel (thumbs up), has a quick, explosive personality (TNT), many hidden talents (locked trunk), a loyal dog (Snowy, his dog), knowledge (book), likes clean living (upturned liquor bottle), has a great-hearted kindness and love of justice (heart), the ability to be amazed, ask questions, and make quick plans of action (thought bubble).

CHARACTER SYMBOL MAPS.

Maps of character values before and after a story can be powerful ways to show character change. I recently asked my students to create such maps for the character Eustace after a reading of C.S. Lewis's *Voyage of the Dawn Treader*. I prompted them to justify the values they identified with evidence from the text. At the end they explained what events were most important in Eustace's transformation.

CHARACTER WARDROBE/ FASHION SHOW.

Teacher Kathy Salkaln has her students create character wardrobes from drawings or magazine cutouts and asks them to explain how this wardrobe shows the character's values, social class, historical period, or inner traits. This could, of course, also lead to dress-up book reports or dress-up tea parties for characters from the same or different texts.

Understanding
Settings, Events, and Ideas

Settings, situations, events and ideas are used by authors to advance their message. Authors of all texts make choices about what details to include, highlight, or describe in a text. They make these choices strategically for the purpose of communicating and promoting particular ideas to their readers.

This next set of techniques delves into understanding situations and settings, and the ideas the author is portraying through them. We will look at the first, tableaux, in several variations.

TABLEAUX

Tableau—a French term for a scene that captures the sweep of a significant moment—has been a favorite technique of mine for a long time. A tableau is versatile, and kids quickly grasp its various uses. I often use tableaux as a drama technique in which groups create "body pictures" or statues with physical stances and gestures that portray story events, relationships, or thematic meanings. I also use this as a visual art technique, which I describe here.

Though I sometimes have students create a single tableau, I more often have them work together to create a series of tableaux that requires them to choose and represent key details, see relationships and patterns across details and scenes, and summarize the whole coherence of ideas presented through a particular text segment.

To make tableaux more purposeful, I usually have the groups who are creating them read different texts than the rest of the class, or I make them experts by

Though tableaux typically do not include text, summaries can be added to create an abridged Big Book/Picture Book version of the story or major idea. (See page 152).

having them focus their tableaux on a particular part, idea, or motif from a shared class reading. The group must consider what it is the rest of the class must know from this text and how to best depict it so their audience will learn and remember useful information.

For example, during a Civil War unit, groups read different stories from various perspectives. A group reading the story "The Soldier Who Wouldn't Tell" created five scenes that summarized the tale and presented them to the rest of the class. I asked them to conclude their presentation with a statement of what the meaning of the story was and how this made a comment on the Civil War.

The students struggled a bit to express a statement so I asked them if there was a theme running across each of the pictures they had created. Here is an excerpt of their conversation, which shows how the tableaux work encourages students to start talking about ideas and themes:

"Sam [Davis] never questioned what was the right thing to do, and he stuck with it...I would totally disagree with him [i.e., with Sam's unswerving devotion to the Confederate cause and his sense of loyalty to a Union traitor]," said Josh.

Sharon added, "Maybe that was the problem. I admired Sam a lot, and I showed that in my picture, but the story showed how no one would budge from his beliefs that really came from where they grew up. And that their state was more important to them then being in the U.S. Funny and weird. But that is probably why there was a war."

"Yeah, no one would compromise," Elisha agreed.

This led to a discussion as to whether and when compromise is a good thing, and when it cannot be accepted. Was Sam Davis in a situation where he could not compromise? The students decided that he was.

"If he had, he couldn't have gone back to his family," Josh opined. "Wow!" remarked Sharon. "This is really helping me understand why the Civil War happened."

On the next page, you'll find a reproducible guide that takes students step by step through the process of creating a tableaux. Feel free to adapt it as you wish.

Summary of "The Soldier Who Wouldn't Tell"

In this true story from the Civil War, retold by George Morrill, Tennessee volunteer Sam Davis is enlisted as a spy to help the Confederacy overcome the Union siege of Vicksburg. Sam obtains sensitive documents from a Union authority who secretly sympathizes with the South. Sam's mother sews the documents into his shoes, and he rides off to deliver the important materials to his generals but is caught by Union pickets. They rip open his shoes and find the documents, and Sam is sentenced to be hanged as a spy. But a Union general is so impressed with his loyalty and integrity that he begs Sam to reveal the traitor who gave him the documents, saying, "He is not worth losing your life for." But Sam refuses, thinking this would be a betrayal of trust and of his cause. The offer is repeated on the gallows; Sam again refuses and is hanged.

A tableaux of the penultimate scene of the story.

TABLEAUX DIRECTIONS FOR NARRATIVE TEXTS

WORKING IN GROUPS:

1 Choose the text or text segment that you wish to depict and visually share with your audience.

2 Consider why the audience will be interested in the text you have read and what they will need to know about it.

3 Review the important scenes and details your audience will need to know from each scene. Please consider the journalist's five W's and H (Who, What, Where, When, Why, and How). Remember that the author signals us to notice particular scenes: the first and last ones, those that are surprising, ones that signal a climax or change in direction, those that offer new and important information, ones that are different in some way, and those that are described in great detail.

CHALLENGE:
USE AS FEW DETAILS OR SCENES AS POSSIBLE TO COMMUNICATE THE WHOLE STORY OR MEANING OF A TEXT.

4 Brainstorm how to present these scenes visually in a way that will communicate all the important details of the scene to the audience.

5 Create visual depictions of the scenes on newsprint sheets. Make notes on the back about what you need to point out to the audience about each scene. For example, you might include a topic word, write a one-sentence summary of the scene, explain how this scene connects to a prior or following tableau, point out key details and explain how these details are important, cite the theme, or deep meaning, of the scene, or relate this theme to the topic of the excerpt.

6 When you are done with your individual tableau, check to be sure that your audience will completely understand and "see" that whole section of the text.

7 When all of your group's tableaux are done, make sure that they work together to show the shape of a story, the stages of the process, or the whole shape of the ideas presented.

8 Rehearse your presentation as a group, making sure everyone is involved.

9 Present it!

10 Get feedback on how well you did and what you could do to improve your presentation.

Teacher Allison Pomerville's elaborated tableaux with music idea.

IDEA TABLEAUX

Tableaux lend themselves particularly well to helping students remember and recreate scenes from a narrative. However, tableaux can also depict more abstract textual elements, such as main ideas, motifs, or themes. They can be used to amplify the ideas or text structures of fiction and nonfiction texts or any other kind of non-narrative text. Students can be assigned an excerpt and asked to depict a major point that the reader must carry away from that excerpt. Students can create characters that personify a concept, such as greed or competition or patience and invent contexts or settings in order to personalize and communicate the meaning of informational texts.

SLIDE SHOWS.

Students can use Powerpoint or Kid Pix to make simple slideshows of tableaux. These can be very sparse and symbolic, or highly detailed and realistic. Just as a traveler wants to show the key places and events of a trip to her friends, students creating these slideshows will depict the central scenes or ideas from a text. Their slideshows will convey the important sights and seminal experiences that capture the essence of their reading experience. They might even animate or blend the scenes together to give the audience a dynamic sense of their journey through a text. These slideshows scaffold readers' consideration of key details; as they share them with each other, they discuss why certain details are key, what needs to be included, and what is lost if a particular slide is deleted. In this way, the kids learn a lot from each other about identifying key details and creating summaries.

FLOW CHARTS.

Having students create flow charts is a very versatile activity that can be used to depict complicated sequences, causal relationships, character development, and the development of various historical trends, debates, or ideas. Flow charts can pictorially show sequence and cause and effect. They can also help students to see the various possibilities—the "what ifs" and choices made at particular times, e.g. flow charts can also explore "roads not taken."

MAPS.

This next idea comes from Peter Smagorinsky's excellent book *Expressions* (1991). Have students make maps of physical locales as small as a room or as large as the country in which a story or text events take place. Students might also make maps of characters' physical,

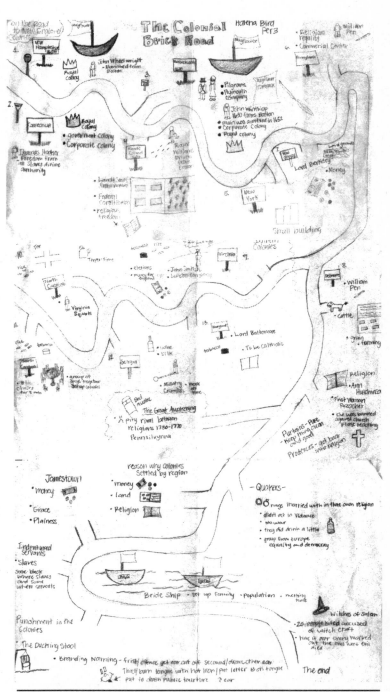

Halena Bird's flow chart displays what she learned about the colonial experience in America. "This is so much better than a test," she commented. "I can see that I understand it, and the drawing helped me to understand it even more. I'm going to remember this!"

GREAT BOOKS

Other historical texts that use primary documents, photos and drawings include:

Anne Frank: Beyond the Diary, by Ruud Van Der Rol,et al. Ancillary materials and documents about Anne's life.

At Her Majesty's Request, by Walter Dean Myers. True story of an African Princess who was Queen Victoria's ward, contrasts different cultural views of leadership, etc.

The Planet Hunters, by Dennis Trodin Franklin. Explores the discovery of Pluto.

Where the Action Was, Penny Colman. Women War Correspondents in WWII.

Shipwreck at the Bottom of the World, by Jennifer Armstrong. Shackleton's amazing voyage of survival.

Through My Eyes, by Ruby Bridges. Multiple perspectives on correspondent Ruby Bridges.

We Were There Too! by Phillip Hoose. Children's role in American history with archival illustrations.

psychological, or spiritual journeys. In the case of quests, Peter asks students to visually depict the sort of terrain over which the hero journeys (this could of course be metaphorical or symbolic), the major events, the sequence of events and how one led to another, and the direction in which the hero travels. He also uses a "mirror map" strategy by asking students to visually depict their own life quest and compare this to that of the hero.

ROLL MOVIES.

Though electronic video technologies and iMovies can do the same thing as old-fashioned roll movies, students often enjoy creating a version or timeline of a story's events on a single sheet. They can then run this sheet as a scroll through a homemade shoe box viewer

DETECTIVE SKETCHES.

My long-time team-teaching partner, Paul Friedemann, likes to assign different students to be "police artists" to do detective sketches as they read. The police artist's job is to recreate a past event or series of events, or sketch out what a suspect looks like based on the available text details. By compiling the sketches made by various students over the course of a text, or the study of an event (like the battle of Gettysburg and its aftermath), a class winds up with a tableau book that features a story's major characters, scenes, or points. Students greatly enjoy this detective work, and this activity highlights the importance of using background information to make inferences and then to revise ideas based on newly presented information.

Paul likes to show students important primary texts and historical documents like Sneden's *Eye of the Storm* (2000) to illustrate how observers of historical events—in this case, a private in the Union army—contribute to our understanding through diaries, sketches, pictures, illustrations, and more.

Some young adult and children's books that fit such a unit are Jim Murphy's *The Boys' War* and *Road to Gettysburg*, Clinton Cox's *Fiery Vision: The Life and Death of John Brown*, and Raymond Bial's *Underground Railroad*, which introduces a different view of John Brown than that offered in Cox's book.

Studying Illustrated Texts

Carefully selected cartoons, picture books, and other illustrated texts can be used to teach many reading strategies, from understanding and visualizing key details to inferring character to understanding irony and symbolism. For example, in Ludwig Bemelman's well-loved *Madeline* books, settings are depicted with colorful tableaux while actions are shown with line drawings. When I show these books to students, I ask: What is important for an illustrator to depict? What can be imagined? How much must be depicted? What cues does the viewer or reader

need to be able to fill in the blanks? What do we need to know to imagine a setting versus imagining a character? How do different techniques work to convey different story aspects? Discussions around such questions help students to not only attend and critically appreciate illustrations, but to think about them in a writerly way—as a method of communication.

Janet Stevens' book *Tops and Bottoms* explores the Brer Rabbit story in a calendar format. Students can study the effect of her playful line work, and how the calendar framing structures their experience of the text. Her book *From*

Pictures to Words: a Book About Making a Book looks at the choices authors and illustrators make in creating a book.

In *To Fly: The Story of the Wright Brothers*, W. Old uses a variety of visual techniques to show the brothers' collaboration, experimentation, moods, and the settings and salient elements of context in which they worked.

ILLUSTRATING TEXTS.

My students enjoy providing illustrations for a nonillustrated text. This technique helps them to visualize from print—to notice and flesh out important details and scenes. Sometimes I ask the class to provide illustrations for a chapter or for a whole text. Their job is to decide what is important in the assigned excerpt and what are the most effective ways to visually highlight this important information. I have always had students draw pictures, flow charts, graphs, and other visuals, but now that I have computers and a digital camera, I also encourage them to stage photographs, dress them up with Adobe PhotoShop, and create other computer graphics.

SUMMARY TEXTS WITH ILLUSTRATED COMMENTARY.

To help students summarize and bring accrued meanings forward, I often have them create summaries of texts they have read independently to share with each other. I sometimes prompt them to create illustrated sidebar commentaries for the categories *frightening facts*, *definitions*, *culture corner*, *Did you know?*, *related statistics*, *related readings*, and *implied social action projects*.

PICTURE BOOK SUMMARIES/BIG BOOKS.

The task of boiling a longer and more complex text down into a picture book helps students to conceive of how to summarize and visually represent ideas from more complicated texts. I've often arranged for my students to adopt reading buddies from lower grades who they meet with and tutor on various occasions throughout the year. This context makes creating a picture book very real for them; their job is to summarize something they've learned for their reading buddy in a way that stimulates interest and helps the younger student to comprehend a story or idea. Students have created excellent summaries of not only stories but also sophisticated concepts, like Newton's laws of motion.

Students can also create what I call "big books"—large picture book summaries. These are alternative versions that might be an iteration from an alternate perspective, an elaboration or extension of a story, or a satire, recasting, or otherwise "twisted" version of a text. Students enjoy inserting themselves and their friends into a text as characters or commentators, which adds the human dimension and connection everyone seeks in reading.

Heather adds various forms of Illustrated commentary and sidebars to her summary of the story *Bright Morning*.

Understanding Inferencing
and Other Skills With Comics

I always have at least some students who are comic book fans. Using comics in the classroom allows them to use a literacy resource from their lives and also provides an opportunity for them to share their expertise with others. Kids often

don't understand the complexity of what they need to do as readers. A constant focus on decoding oversimplifies reading and may lead kids away from complex reading strategies like inferencing. Texts like comics make the necessity of these strategies obvious, with their breaks between panels, which are inferencing gaps known as "gutters."

There are now many sophisticated comic books that teach complex content-area concepts from economics, mathematics, science, and history. A quick browse of your local bookstore or Amazon.com can give you plenty of texts to use. Japanese comics, a current craze among middle-schoolers, often use few words and incredible renderings of action and setting to tell stories. All of these comics can be used in a variety of creative ways, as described below.

TEACHING INFERENCING

The gutters, or spaces between comic panels, are in fact very concrete examples of "inference gaps." Readers must provide the transitions or missing information between the panels to create a coherent text. Comics can therefore be used to help students understand Umberto Eco's notion that in any kind of reading, the author provides us with point A and point E, and it is up to us to take "inferential walks" that lead us from A, creating for ourselves points B, C, and D to make sure we end up at point E.

When we look at comics together, I ask my students to describe the panel-to-panel action. As they "fill in the gutter," offering plot points and other details that are not shown, I ask them to justify their elaborations. Another technique is to copy comics with a panel missing, and ask students to supply the action in the missing panel. This variation allows students to see how different authorial choices lead to different meanings.

TEACHING TEXT-SPECIFIC (GENRE) CONVENTIONS.

Comics generally consist of four panels which correspond to narrative structure: exposition, complication, climax, and resolution/comment/punch line. Students can create comic strips to recapture the sequence of any kind of plot, text structure, or conceptual presentation. For example, they might follow any of these structures:

- ◆ **Compare and contrast:** The first panel depicts what is being compared and why, the second panel shows similarities, the third panel shows differences, and the fourth offers a conclusion.
- ◆ **Basic argument:** Successive panels show the claim, a compelling piece of evidence, a warrant, and a conclusion.
- ◆ **Definition:** Panel one introduces the term; panel two contains examples of the idea; panel three shows nonexamples; panel four offers a definition, and uses of the definition.
- ◆ **Summary:** Single-panel comics, like those of the famous *Far Side*, are a kind of tableaux that is great for summarizing the central point of a story.

My friend Jamie Heans asks his students to translate comic strips into dramatic scripts before they start to read a play. In this way, they learn about speaker designation, stage directions, setting directions, character directions, and more. All of these are conventions of scripts that do not exist in any other kind of text. Doing this several times helps Jamie's students to understand that when they read a script, they are being prompted to visualize settings and characters; to hear characters speaking, see where they are standing, and perceive what they are doing.

TEACHING SYMBOLISM AND IRONY.

Task-specific conventions are those that can be found in any kind of text type but which go well beyond the general processes that are necessary to read any kind of text. Symbolism and irony are examples of such conventions. Comics are particularly good at teaching different forms of symbolism and irony and how to read these forms. Comics are usually meant to be funny and often turn on irony. Kids can also be asked to create cartoons that express irony.

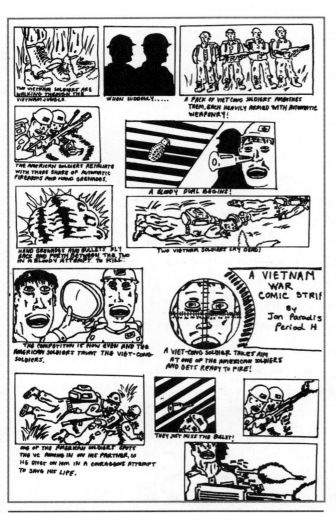

A comic book summary of a story from Tim O'Brien's collection *The Things They Carried.*

We need to help students understand that irony requires us to recognize a literal or expected meaning, and then an implied or alternative meaning that subverts the literal. Michael Smith (1989) explains that the reader of irony needs to understand the literal meaning and recognize that there is an implied alternate meaning by noticing the following tip-offs (from Booth, 1974):

- A straightforward warning that we might need to read carefully or that we shouldn't believe everything we read.

- A speaker in the text proclaims a known error (thereby distancing the author from the speaker).

- There is a conflict between what an individual character thinks and what he says or does. There is a conflict of belief between characters, or a character believes something we find hard to justify.

- There is a clash of style; some information is presented in a different way stylistically.

After noticing any of the above tip-offs, we need to take these four steps:

- ◆ Reject the surface meaning.
- ◆ Decide what is not under dispute that we can believe.
- ◆ Apply our knowledge of the world to generate a reconstructed meaning that makes more sense.
- ◆ Check our reconstructed meaning against our knowledge of the world, the author, other books, and so on, as far as we are able. Ask, Does this now make sense?

In this Julius Caesar cartoon the soothsayer proclaims a known error. His drinking also codes him as unreliable. This is an ironic commentary on the play, in which the soothsayer is reliable, but is not believed, and the result is the same.

COMIC WEBSITES

For ideas on using comics, there is a great New Zealand website: english.unitecnology. ac.nz/resources/units/ home.html

Searching for "comics" on this site results in a range of material, including a unit on creating cartoons, guidelines for studying social and political cartoon satire, comic book resources, electronic comics, and links to clip art and cartoon sites. Also search www.discover.tased.ed u.au/english/, where you will also find a range of ideas for studying comics (including critical literacy strategies) and examples of teachers using cartoons across the curriculum.

FLOOR PLANS/SETTING MANDALAS.

To help students visualize complete settings, have them find or create a map of a setting from a text. I also often ask them to create a floor plan of an important room or setting so that they can be helped to visualize events and interactions in that space. Sometimes we even recreate such an imaginary space in our classroom.

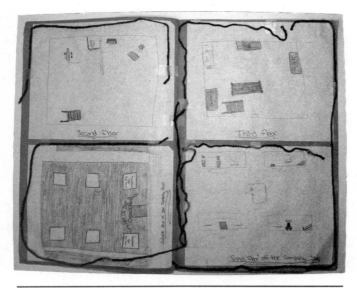

Creating floor plans and room maps can help the reader visualize scenes and move imaginatively through these "story spaces."

PHOTO SCAVENGER HUNT.

Teacher Brooke Merow provides students with digital cameras and sets them off on scavenger hunts to find settings, images, symbols, buildings, visual patterns, and situations that parallel elements from a story they are reading. For example, when studying repetition and parallelism, Brooke asked students to bring in repeated and parallel images. They discussed the effects of this kind of imaging, and then talked about how this technique is also used in writing. When studying contrast and juxtaposition, she asked them to take or find pictures in which very different shapes or figures were contrasted. Again, effects and parallel writing techniques were discussed.

Student photographs can be used to teach about the effect of various constructions like compare-contrast.

STORY COLLAGES.

Teacher Jane Chamberlain uses story collages to prompt students to attend to particular story elements, like major characters, significant events, and settings. But she also often prompts them to include important details or motifs, the author's meaning, the reader's response to the story, something they visualized that was not explicitly stated, or a visual relating the text to another text from the unit they are engaged in. Many of these prompts assist students with inferencing.

Because it can often imply something deep and abstract through the concrete and superficial, poetry is considered condensed, imagistic, nuanced, and referential. Perhaps because of this, my students often have great difficulty reading and understanding poetry. After a visit to a neighboring school, however, one of them—Becky—came up with a helpful idea for understanding poems. Her idea was to make poetry collages, which can be used to do several different things. Students can be

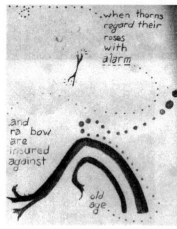

Joanna's picture book of ee cumming's "When Serpents Squirm"

...valleys accuse their

mountains

of having

altitude –

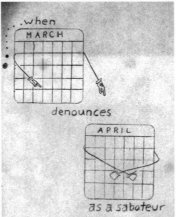

...when
MARCH

denounces

APRIL

as a saboteur

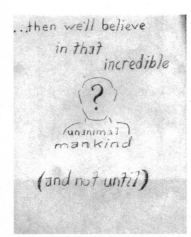

...then we'll believe

in that

incredible

?

(unanimal)
mankind

(and not until)

About the Author

More of Joanna's picture book.

asked to create each image suggested by the poem or an image for each line or section. Or they might create a collage of images directly suggested by the poem on the left side of a posterboard, put the poem itself in the middle, and then make a collage of their response on the right. Their responses might include what they construe to be the implied, or deep meaning, of the poem, a personal response, or information about a current world situation that the poem prompts them to consider.

Bringing Life
to Literature

The techniques explored in this chapter are meant to assist students to visualize the landscape of character, action, event and situation. But because of the very nature of reading as a transactional pursuit in which we bring our own needs, questions and experiences to bear in conversation with a text, these techniques also prompt students to bring their life experience to their meaning-making conversations with a text. This stimulates students to make inferences and to begin searching for deeper implied meanings that reside in the textual conversation.

These techniques also encourage students to mark and display their own identity and values, often in relationship or opposition to a text. This is something students, like all human beings, desire and value. But it is also something that is typically denied them in school (Smith and Wilhelm, 2002).

One of the most beautiful poetry collages I have ever seen was my seventh grade student Tanya's poster of Shel Silverstein's poem "This Bridge Will Take you Half Way There". (The poster was unfortunately thrown away by an overzealous custodian.)

Tanya created half a beautiful bridge made of wild scaffolds. This, she explained, was "the text the author offers to me. It gets you started on your reading journey." In the center of the poster, poised on the end of the bridge as if it were a diving board overhanging the abyss was a picture of herself, poised to dive. Thought bubbles emanated from her head, the ones closest to her imagined the rest of the bridge, using various different materials and construction ideas. "This is me," she explained, "imagining how I want to finish the story, which I have to do, because the text only 'takes you half way there'. You have to finish it on your own. I'm thinking the author wants me to finish the bridge using his own construction ideas, but I am going to bring my own ideas, so even though the bridge will take me over to the other side, it will do so in the way that fits my needs, to help me see 'those wonderful worlds' I want to see." On the far right side of the poster were thought bubbles of the imagined settings and events Tanya wanted to experience. "The story is half the author's," she claimed, "and half mine. We make it together." I was astounded! It was a perfect demonstration and explanation of transactional reader response theory from a seventh grader!

This is a powerful recommendation for visual strategies. All of the techniques explored here can be used to help students bring themselves to texts, to stake their own identities and values, and to not only understand authors, but to embrace and oppose them in different ways, and to build on texts to create connections to themselves and the world they live in.

CHAPTER 7

Moving Past
Main Ideas

*Identifying, Placeholding, and Interpreting
Key Ideas to Create Knowledge*

*S*ometimes even the most
unreflective teacher is
taught a lesson that
can't be shrugged off. It
happened to me once when I'd spent
a miserable year that had fallen on
me like a ton of bricks. During that
year I spent a lot of extra time in the
shower, contemplating taking sick
days and switching professions.

I'd been sent from the high school to the middle school to teach a load including two classes of eighth-grade remedial reading. Initially I thought it was a demotion—that I had been sent "down" to the middle school. In retrospect, it was the best thing that ever happened to me as a teacher. But I still imagine that first year as a series of Batman sounds: YOW! and KAPOW! and OOFF! I was simply getting beaten up.

The problem was that my students resisted everything. One of them, Danny, told me: "I ain't never read, I ain't never going to read, and you can't make me." A few kids did actually cooperate perfunctorily with a lesson or two, but there was no real engagement. Most of my students refused to do anything, while many actively resisted, telling me how stupid each assignment was: "This is boring." "This is crap!" "How is this going to help us?"

I tried behavior programs, detentions, lectured them on responsibility, provided rewards and punishments galore—all techniques befitting a curriculum-centered behavioristic approach (Kohn, 1996). Out of desperation, I began to experiment wildly. For the first time, I did some pre-assessments and interest inventories: I began interviewing kids about their school and reading experiences. I asked them directly why they hated school and reading and my class so much. In fact, this was the beginning of my journey as a teacher researcher, only I didn't know it. All I knew is that I was stunned by answers I got. They gave me a glimmer of understanding that my students might be right, that the activities I assigned were not connected to their current needs or the realities of their foreseeable futures.

Still desperate, I chose new materials and we started reading magazines, children's books, and young adult literature about topics "closer to home." This was the first time I used S.E. Hinton's *The Outsiders* and *That Was Then, This Was Now*. Though certainly not unqualified successes, they were my most engaging units. I began to think systematically about what seemed to work and what didn't, what students would resist and what they would try. I asked them to help me, and some of them did. Others, like Tricia, would respond to each request with the comment, "You are such a loser!"

Even after making a little progress, I was still demoralized. But I realized that the kids were even more demoralized, and that while I had some power to help them, they had little power to help me or themselves. They were caught in a system that did not work or make sense for them.

STARTING FROM SCRATCH

The next year, I jumped at the chance to join an integrated teaching team. It had to be better than what I'd just been through. The team was organized as the EEN house (exceptional educational needs) and we had all of the labeled kids (LD, ED, ADHD, ESL) in a mainstreamed situation. Our job was to find a way to usefully teach all of the students together.

With this group, my education as a teacher continued. I had learned to listen to kids, and I had found some great colleagues. The one to whom I owe more than I can say is Paul Friedemann, who became my team teaching partner for six years in the EEN house. He helped me think through things, and he always had the energy and vision to want to try something new to solve the myriad problems that came up. When something didn't go well, he'd say, "Jeff, let's change it! We have the power!" Paul has the consummate teacher researcher attitude: "If something is broken, let's fix it. If something is going well, let's make it even better."

We struggled together, and at the end of the first year, Paul told me that he was ready to start from scratch. "School doesn't make sense to these kids! Our classes don't make sense," he told me. "We have to redo things so they make sense to the kids or we will never get anywhere!"

So we agreed to rethink everything—our purposes, our theories, our assignments, our techniques, even our schedule (we shared the same kids for five periods and ended up blocking classes in a nonblocked school). At the same time, I was taking classes at the University of Wisconsin from Rich Lehrer, a leading cognitive scientist. Rich was tremendously helpful to us and generous with his time. He is also a proponent of "learning by inquiry and design" (Lehrer, 1993) and "learning by understanding" (Wiggins and McTighe, 2001). Both of these teaching models are based squarely on the sociocultural learning-centered theory.

Paul and I decided to try the inquiry frame for teaching. We superimposed it over the curriculum we were required to teach, basically addressing the same material by reorganizing it into integrated themes and reframing it with a new orientation and purpose. We were surprised at how all the essential ideas we had been covering in a curriculum-centered way actually fit into inquiry themes that allowed student activity to be purposeful—allowing them to achieve deep foundational understandings.

Our attempt started off slow, with an initial five-day unit on designing personality profiles on hyperstacks for a unit on personal identity. Throughout the next couple of years, we corresponded constantly with Rich Lehrer, and he visited our school several times. Three years later, everything we did was inquiry driven, organized around four quarter-long inquiry units that addressed all the designated curriculum material. Our students were thriving, and we were enjoying them and each other. Hey, even test scores were going up. Life was good.

Becoming Authors of Knowledge

This book has been about using visuals to create meaning in concert with textual information. Now it moves on to discussing visuals to placehold information so that it can be operated on—added to, analyzed, critiqued, and used. Previous chapters were about fleshing out and enlivening textual information by using visuals to help students transact with the text. Many techniques were shared that can be used to frame a purposeful inquiry context (frontloading), and that will help students discern and placehold the information offered in a text (tableaux, timelines, the central focus sequence). In this chapter, I offer some further techniques for discerning the main ideas of particular texts through the use of visual tools. But I do so in the context of inquiry, of helping students to see various patterns and perspectives across texts and situations, so that deep understandings can be achieved. I move to helping students to operate on and interpret visually represented information for the purpose of analyzing and using what has been learned. And finally, I show how visuals can be used as the media for "authoring" and "designing" knowledge, as students represent what they are learning and have learned.

Rich Lehrer's research into classroom inquiry demonstrates that most of what is called "inquiry" simply involves copying information from sources. As a result, it often produces plagiarism. Further, the end point is usually a simple report or project, not the use, application, or extension of information. In true inquiry, students cannot plagiarize because the point is not to recapitulate information; the point is to go beyond what is currently known and to create a unique and usable "knowledge artifact." Such learning is problem-based. Problems animate our learning in the world because we must use the knowledge we gain by making a decision or taking action to solve them . In problem-solving, students must know the various perspectives about an issue and then choose, adapt, and develop new ways of using these perspectives.

The concept of "usability" is important to David Perkins's notion of "knowledge," which he differentiates from "information" (1991). In the chart on the next page, I differentiate the concepts of information and knowledge.

Perkins (1991) posits that knowledge is distinguished by is structuredness, systematicity, applicability, and extensibility. Information does not share any of these features. Based on recent advances in cognitive psychology and literacy, I've added some additional contrasts between information and knowledge in the chart on the next page.

Throughout this chapter, I attempt to show how the visual strategies recommended throughout the whole of this book are forms of knowledge construction and representation rather than ways to purvey "factual" information. The process of reading, finding relevant information, seeing connections and patterns across information sources, developing missing information, and shaping the accrued knowledge into usable knowledge artifacts is the very process of inquiry and designing knowledge. This chapter focuses on using visuals to find, placehold, and analyze major ideas. In the end, students should be able to see with, think with, and use these major ideas.

Information	Knowledge
is received from outside sources	is socially and culturally constructed; must involve personal effort, contributions, and connection-making to be internalized by an individual
may not involve a mental model	involves creating a new mental model (to the learner) for understanding a concept, process, or genre
is usually decontextualized; taught separately from use	is always contextualized—learned and applied in a situation in which the knowledge is required and used
is recapitulated	is transformed, transmediated, re-represented in new ways
is submitted or sometimes displayed (e.g., homework)	is usable over time by self and others; can be adapted and transferred to new situations
is "schoolish"—only counts in school contexts	is "toolish"—can help to perform tasks and extend human abilities in the world outside of school
is completed and then discarded (e.g., term papers, tests)	is archival and extensible over time, by creator and others; can be continually revised and built upon
is fragmented	is structured and systematic—there is a clear relationship and interplay between structure, details, and use
is linear	is weblike—data is interconnected within and across sources, like Internet hotlinks
is established, inert, static	is generative, additive, dynamic, evolving, revisable
is accepted, unjustified	is justified—reasoning is made visible and accountable—and reservations are acknowledged and responded to
is considered to be "factual"	is considered to be socially constructed and therefore revisable, extensible, and so on.
is the end of learning	Finding information is the beginning of learning.
Teaching is the donation of information to learners.	Teaching is assisting learners in learning and problem-solving performances with data and strategies for the end of constructing deep understandings.
Knowing involves the *what*; memorization and recapitulation of information	Knowing involves the *why, how* and *what*, in that order of priority. Human purposes for the knowledge is foregrounded.
The purpose of learning is telling back.	Learning is the application of knowledge, which continues to develop and evolve throughout life as it is applied to new situations.

Picture Mapping

One of the most versatile visualization techniques I've ever used is picture mapping, an idea I learned 20 years ago from the CRISS Project (Content Reading in Secondary Schools). Basic picture mapping involves identifying and summarizing in pictures the key ideas of a textual passage. To bring picture mapping in line with how readers identify key details and add together their meanings, I've added the requirements that students identify the topic and create a pictorial topic representation. I also ask that they consider the meaning that accrues from the relationships between the details to come up with a central focus/main idea that they also represent visually. The picture map then provides a powerful visual summary of the topic (what general subject all the key details address).

An essential element of text comprehension is understanding how ideas are patterned throughout a text. As introduced in Chapter 6, there are six basic ways in which text details are organized to create meaning through their relationships:

1. **Stated relationships.** Authors identify the relationship between details; e.g., in *Roll of Thunder*, that Mr. Morrison's huge size was caused by white slave owner's breeding the biggest slaves together over the course of generations.

2. **Simple implied relationships.** Authors put related ideas close together in a text, assuming that readers will see the connections; e.g., that Cassie's beating of Lillian Jean was on her body, not her face, because of warnings Papa had given her earlier in the book.

3. **Complex implied relationships.** These are more challenging patterns of meaning in which the reader is asked to infer the meaning of details far apart from each other and stretched across a text. This may include textual gaps which the author expects readers to be able to fill in. For example, in *Roll of Thunder*, consider what happens between Uncle Hammer and Mr. Morrison in Uncle Hammer's car. Readers are given the initial details of Uncle Hammer's resolve to confront Charlie Simms (that would certainly end in a lynching), and the details of their return home the next morning. We must infer from the available details that Mr. Morrison must have

talked Uncle Hammer out of going to the Simmses.

4. **Authorial generalization.** This is the point made by the accumulated relationships of details throughout a text; e.g., in *Roll of Thunder* the results of fighting injustice in various ways show that using your intelligence to fight in subtle ways using the law and the existing system is more effective than direct assaults through physical force or the use of emotions.

5. **Local text structure patterns.** These are patterns for organizing details that are embedded into a text at a local level. Such structural patterns include simple listing, time order (chronology), cause and effect, compare-contrast, classification, and definition.

Picture maps can show how historical ideas developed over time or how story ideas relate to create meaning.

6. **Global/genre and text structure patterns.** These are superstructure patterns that organize a whole text, give it coherence, and provide an overall roadmap for reading. Some of the same patterns that work locally can also organize a whole text, e.g. compare-contrast, classification, extended definition, and narrative chronology. Other generic superstructure patterns include argument, ironic monologue, fable, and dramatic script.

BASIC
PICTURE MAPPING DIRECTIONS

(1) Have students work in groups of three or four to complete a picture map. This size group is small enough so that everyone will be involved but large enough that there will be an exchange of ideas and discussion. Instruct groups to:

(2) Read through the text excerpt.

(3) Identify the topic of the reading (the general subject that all major ideas or events share in common) and create a pictorial representation of it.

(4) Go through the text and mark or list each key idea about the topic, paying attention to the key detail clues including:

- First and last sentences of the text because introductions and conclusions often signal the topic and key ideas about it
- Paragraph breaks, which often signal a new key idea
- First and last sentences of paragraphs
- Highlights, boldface, italics, bullets, boxes, and font changes, all of which signal attention to key ideas
- Quoted material
- Surprises, shifts, and changes in focus, direction, or emphasis

(5) Consider how to represent or symbolize each key idea with a picture or symbol—as simply and clearly as they can!

(6) Identify how the key details work together to create a deep meaning and statement about the world outside the text. This is the central focus statement (also known as a main idea or thematic generalization). Consider how to represent this main idea in a single picture.

ADVANCED PICTURE MAPPING IDEAS

- Add to each key detail picture how you knew that each key detail was essential and didn't just provide texture.

- Demonstrate several key ideas with one picture or symbol.

- Show the patterns and connections between ideas or progressions of ideas if the organization and structure of the text is important to the point it makes (e.g., Organize the picture map into a timeline if there is historical cause and effect, into a family tree if it involves relationships or classes of information, Venn diagrams if it involves definition or compare-contrast.

- Add a response corner (could also be done on the back of the picture map) depicting your response to the text and your feelings about the information presented and issues raised. Indicate what surprised you, what you want to do as a result of this reading, and so on. You could even draw a picture of yourself thinking about the text, showing to what degree you accept, would adapt, or resist the message and implications for thinking and living provided by the text. If several of you worked on the picture map together,

you could each use a corner for your individual responses.

- Use a picture map to summarize the whole unit. Be sure to show the key details across various texts and experiences, how they relate to each other, and the conclusion (big understandings/central foci) you gleaned from the unit as a whole.

- Show your picture map to another group. Let them guess what each symbol/picture and the various placements/relationships mean.

- Use your picture map to show students in other groups what was important about your text. If individuals or groups are reading different texts for the same inquiry unit, make sure your picture map is strong enough that they will know the most important things you learned about the inquiry topic so they can think with these ideas, too.

- Use your picture map to study for a test, write a paper, or just to jog your memory. How well does it work in meeting these purposes?

- Hang the picture maps in the classroom and use them as references for writing assignments, tests, and discussions.

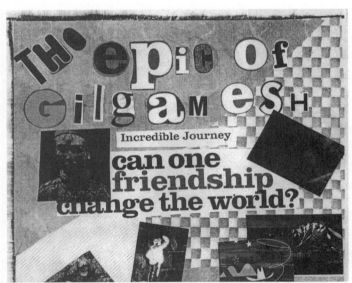

Picture maps provide a powerful visual summary of the topic (what all the key details have in common), the key details themselves, the structured relationships of ideas, and the central focus. This process of creating them helps students to deeply understand how text structures work to develop and express particular meanings. Understanding this as a reader aids students to organize texts as writers (Hillocks, 1986).

PICTURE MAPPING ADAPTATIONS

Often the thematic meaning of a story, or even a history, hinges on how a situation or a character is changed by the events in the narrative. In this case, a Before and After picture map allows students to analyze and see the patterns of change, so that they can draw conclusions about general principles of being and acting in the world. Cause and effect relationships can be added by

Picture maps comparing the experience of characters Brent Bishop of *Whirligig* to Gilgamesh from the Babylonian epic.

connecting before and after values of a character through a map. For example, I recently had students depict the changes in Eustace, from C.S. Lewis's *The Voyage of the Dawn Treader*, that resulted from the challenges, adventures, and

A poetry collage comparing the quests of Brent Bishop and Gilgamesh.

relationships he experienced on his epic voyage. Some students wrote a series of several postcards to create a character-change postcard sequence, which depicted the gradual changes Eustace underwent and how these changes were related to various experiences.

Flow or step charts often work nicely to depict cause and effect, narrative, or process description. In a flow chart, students show how ideas and events relate to each other over time. These can also be extended through the use of mirror mapping techniques, in which students compare and contrast anything through a map (e.g., perspectives). Students might compare their own and an author's or character's values at different points in a story.

For example, teacher Cindy Dean has her students create flow charts of the hero quest archetype during an extended unit in which her students ask, "What is a hero?" and explore structures such as the archetype. She has students create mirror maps comparing archetypal mythological heroes to heroes of today.

Students are expected to show how both the mythological and contemporary heroes share aspects of the archetype, including a sequestered childhood, a special teacher, a loyal sidekick, a special but hidden skill, the undertaking of a challenge that involves a quest, a descent into the underworld or a spiritual encounter, and the aiding of others who benefit from the successful completion of the quest.

PAST-PRESENT FUTURE TRIPTYCH

Cindy also adapts the self/text/world triptych concept so that students can examine cause-and-effect influences on characters, events, policies, and proposals. One panel of the triptych designates an event or quality that was exhibited before the story, the middle panel depicts the current situation, and the final panel shows future events, including possible consequences or possibilities now opened.

FLASHBACK MAPPING

In this activity, students compare current events to those in a story about the past. Paul Fleischman's *Dateline Troy*, in which he compares the events of the Trojan War to analogous modern historical events, can prove an inspiring model for this technique.

Fleischman compares events from current events to those from the Trojan War.

Students could depict a mythological event on one page and a corresponding modern day event on the facing page, as Fleishman does, or even create an extended picture book or hypermedia book that connects a succession of various story events with various modern ones.

Such techniques can be effective any time you want students to make text to text connections or to see points of contact or analogies between different stories (e.g. between the YA novel *America*, and *Great Expectations*), different phenomena (freezing and rigor mortis), different processes (cleaning your house and fasting's effect on the body or growing up in a family and being a colony).

How These Techniques Spark Transformative Discussions

As I walk around while students create picture maps, I always hear similar discussions. They are intensely discussing what the topic might be and how precisely they can identify and represent it. They argue about key details—which are important and which are merely texture. The students help each other to see the patterns of relationships among the details, to discern the trajectory and flow of ideas through a piece, and to highlight examples of these key details.

In particular, they passionately consider the central focus statement. Students always talk at length about how to represent the ideas. For David Quammen's "*Republic of Cockroaches*," they ask "Is this really about cockroaches, or something else that they represent? Like

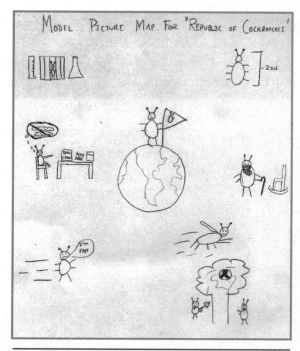

A picture map for David Quammen's "Republic of Cockroaches".

survival, or how species adapt?" "What is the nuclear radiation sign?" "How can we show that cockroaches will eat anything but cucumbers?" "How can we show the cockroach is the oldest creature on the planet?".

These discussions about representing written ideas in visual form involve what semiotic theoreticians call "transmediation." These theorists argue that we create and demonstrate deep understanding by our ability to put ideas into a different form—by putting a written text or picture into our own words; creating a dance or movement expression of a process; or, in this case, putting written text into patterns of visual representations. The power of visual display is often wrapped up in the power of transmediation to transform ideas from information into knowledge. This transformation makes these ideas personally constructed, systematic, structured, extensible, and usable artifacts that we can think and work with.

One of my seventh graders once described his own process of transmediation to his picture mapping group. I'm paraphrasing here, but it was a chant that went like this: "First we have to read it! Then we have to talk it! Then we have to draw it! Then we have to organize it! Then we have to use it! Then we have to share it!"

This is entirely in keeping with Vygotskian ideas about learning. First, all learning is metaphoric, and the new must be connected to the already known; it must be operated on, connected, and transformed into something usable by the learner. Second, for new ideas to be deeply understood, they must be considered from all sides, in all dimensions, and from various perspectives.

There are many other ways of transmediating texts by transforming them into other forms—making excerpts into pictureless books, fable books, flip books, comic books, hypermedia animations, twisted fairy tales, timelines, flow charts, videos, and more. These are not simple projects; they are devices that encourage and demonstrate deep understanding.

QUOTE BOOKS

I enjoy having students create quote books, asking them to collect the most important, revealing quotations from a particular character. I then ask them to create a book of these quotations, including illustrations of their meaning and explanations of their significance.

To get at repeated motifs, themes, and authorial generalizations, this can also be done for a historical figure. For example, I just finished reading David McCullough's Pulitzer Prize-winning biography of John Adams. I was so impressed with John Adams that I went back through the book and pulled out my favorite quotations from his speeches, diaries, and correspondence. Reading these quotes over gave me a great sense of his stance toward life and helped me to know him better in both a personal way and an historical way. I could easily have added visuals to create a quotations book.

The same thing could be done for an author, a character, for one text or across texts. One of my seventh-grade students, Cora, created a book of quotations across the many books she had read by Katherine Paterson. She grouped the quotations around central themes that she discerned in Paterson's work, like the importance of relationship, forgiveness, dealing with death and loss.

Take-offs on quotations books include passage displays, in which a student or students make a poster of the meaning of an important passage from a text or a directly stated central focus. The quoted passage can be the center of the display or be used

A Quote Book from Maya Angelou's *I Know Why the Caged Bird Sings.*

artistically in various ways (broken up into parts repeated) through the artistic display.

QUOTATIONS/POEMS ON THE SUBWAY.

I noticed while riding on the subway that on each car one of the advertising panels was an illustrated line or two from a poem or a quotation from a literary/historical character. (I later discovered it is a campaign in many major U.S. cities called Poetry in Motion, sponsored by Barnes and Noble.) I brought the idea back to school and had my students create illustrated quotations or poems for the hallway in our school.

VISUAL CORRESPONDENCE

In this response activity I ask students to write a postcard or letter exchange between characters or historical figures from textual material they have read. The correspondence must review important information, give personal perspectives on the information and its importance, demonstrate relationships among the characters or historical figures who are corresponding, and perhaps even provide elaborations on the information.

THESE POSTCARDS AND LETTERS CAN BE:

- from a character (or group of characters)
  in one text to a character in another one;
- between two characters from the same text;
- between minor and major characters;
- between unmentioned imaginary characters and characters who might have had an influence on them (an American patriot and King George III, for example);
- from real people to characters and vice versa;
- from you to a character or vice versa.

The postcards require students to imagine an event, setting, or scene and then to communicate their perspective, in role, about this scene to another character.

FROM "THE DAY THEY STOPED THE WAR"

A student in character as Major Cartwright from England, writes a postcard to a German officer about their men's Christmas day soccer match.

As you could see from the front, this is a very disgraceful time. But unfortunately it was the only time there was peace. I don't know how but these men were able to makes peace on Christmas day and the Pope couldn't even do it. It all must be part of Christmas miracles. Too bad it didn't last so everyone would stop the war. Write to me some time after the war. If we live that long.

Hope the war ends soon,
Major Cartwright

FROM *VOYAGE OF THE DAWN TREADER*

Dear Peter,
Narnia is just as I remembered it! Reepicheep, head of the talking mice, is on board! Also is Caspian! As you see on the cover is a picture of what we are sailing into. If the sun looks large to you it is not because I never got around to drawing lessons but because it is larger! Also the water is fresh! We draw it up by the bucket full and drink it, it tastes indescribable! We do not get hungry or tired. Euslace is a brick! He has shaped up after being turned into a dragon. He's quite enjoyable and liked by all. I must go on the poop.   Your Sister, Lucy

Then the receiver must write back. Sometimes kids write both cards; other times I have them exchange, actually responding in role to another student's postcard.

If students exchange letters, I might require them to use visuals through a correspondence poster by posting the two letters on a posterboard, designing appropriate stationery, and illustrating the area around the letters with scenes and events that are described. Or students could provide visual enclosures that are appropriate to their correspondence, such as maps, photographs, drawings, journal pages.

More Ways to Highlight Key Details or Themes

There are many other ideas for highlighting the key details or main ideas in a text. Several teachers I know have students create symbolic borders or picture frames for the visuals they create. These symbolic borders can communicate the meaning of the scene that is depicted, various perspectives on it, the reader's personal response to it, self/world/intra- or intertextual connections to the presented information, uses for the information, and so on.

RESPONSE MAPPING

Another kind of pattern that is useful to track, placehold, and study is that of the individual reader's response (or the response of groups of readers). Students, as kids and as humans, are intensely self-interested. It is interesting, fun, and useful for them to map out their various responses to a text or a series of texts. This, in turn, can serve as a useful springboard for personal exploration and goal-setting, as they try new strategies for sharing responses with each other and deepening understanding of text.

In Phyllis Whitin's excellent book *Sketching Stories, Stretching Minds*, she has students draw pictures of how they read and respond to texts, like mazes or puzzles they were trying to solve, and to use line or pie graphs to summarize the emotional intensity, intellectual engagement, and other features of their response to various parts of the text. Whitin also has students draw their reading and writing processes to study how they work and how they might work more effectively. Students can also be prompted to draw

A scene from Kristy Heller's reading biography in which she explores how she came to detest spelling tests.

parts of a text that are most interesting, scariest, most uplifting, or most thought-provoking.

READING BIOGRAPHIES

I have often had my students create visual reading autobiographies that identify the kind of readers they were at various points in their lives by showing what they read, how they read these things, and how they used and shared their reading so we could all trace their development. Students identify events, books, or situations that affected their attitudes and abilities as readers. These autobiographies can take many forms: pop-up books, picture books, graphic novels, flow charts, or timelines. This project represents a form of personal inquiry into students' own learning processes, and it often lets me understand them in ways that helped me to teach them.

I could share many pages more of visualization ideas, but I imagine you have enough to get immersed in this set of techniques. It's your turn to develop activities of you own! To that end, on the next page I provide guidelines for doing just that.

DESIGNING A
VISUALIZATION TOOL ACTIVITY

When designing visual activities, please demonstrate your understanding of how readers read and respond to literature and other texts and how they "bring meaning forward," learning text by text and activity by activity.

Criteria:

1. Each activity should require students to enter and evoke the world of the text.

2. The activities should encourage students to elaborate on the text world, to fill in gaps, to make inferences, and to extend their reading to making connections beyond the text.

3. The activities should encourage students to revisit textual details and experiences and to reorganize, bring forward, and reflect upon what they have learned.

4. The activities should encourage students to achieve a richer and more "valid" reading of the text—to respectfully attend to and consider all relevant textual details even as they operate on these to make personally significant meanings.

5. The activities should ask students to hone other skills and develop knowledge outside the domain of the text, e.g. learn about interviewing skills, news show formats, review writing, and so on.

6. The activities should be fun for the kids and should ask them to learn something they didn't already know (instead of just revisiting what they already know) and to achieve or practice some new learning processes they have not already mastered.

7. The activities should provide some real-world work; pursuing and completing them should help to teach kids in the class about each other and about the book or unit topic; they should be part of a community service or partner school project; and so on. In any case, the work should be real, have some real-world audiences, and do some kind of "social work."

8. Please display your knowledge of how visual tools can work as a means to assist students' learning performances.

Afterword
To Make Learning Visible

Some students came in to my classroom the other day, completely agitated by a test they had just taken in their geography class. "It was full of tricks!" one girl complained. "Yeah," replied the boy next to her. "He [the teacher] was just trying to trick us into failing!"

I know that a lot of school activity, curriculum-centered as it is, tries to trick kids into failure. From my learning centered perspective, we should be trying to trick students into success by tapping into their strengths to develop new strengths and by providing them with meaningful situations and tools through which they can make meaning in that situation. We should give them multiple ways to be successful and provide them with various tools for exploring, responding, and making meaning.

Bette Manchester, a wonderful principal with whom I worked for several years would say to her teachers: "Your job is to create perceived competencies and perceived autonomy, and the way to do that is to make the kids' learning visible and accountable." I couldn't agree with Bette more, and I know that the tools in this book can help you to do that kind of work.

The only point of any learning activity is to develop new thinking skills and processes that you can use to be better the next time you do something. That has been my aim: to give you tools that you can give your students, so that both of you can be more successful in your work—you at teaching and your students at learning.

And yet the best teaching is a form of learning. That has been the point of the teacher-research subtheme to this book. When we give students tools to make their thinking and reading visible, we can learn from students what they know, how they best learn, and what they need to be helped with next. This makes us better, more responsive, and more professional teachers.

As we engage in this process of observing students and their work, we become reflective practitioners, asking how students learn and how we can help them with their questions and challenges. We observe students so that we can engage them, providing them with the tools they need to do the work they need to do. This is strategic teaching.

Teacher research shifts the relationships in a classroom. Instead of delivering information, we invest ourselves in the creative and relational work of engaging, challenging, and assisting students in new ways. As we do so, we can provide students with tools such as those presented here, that can help them to undertake new relationships as well—with the content they are learning, with themselves as learners, with each other, and with the world. All of this happens when we shift our emphasis from "schoolishness" to "toolishness," from content to strategies, from information to knowledge construction, from ourselves to those we are trying to teach. I hope this book can help you in some way to pursue this all-important work.

Bibliography

WORKS CITED

Armstrong, T. *The Multiple Intelligences of Reading and Writing*. Alexandria, VA: ASCD, 2003.

—. *Multiple Intelligences in the Classroom*. Alexandria, VA: ASCD, 2000.

—. *Seven Kinds of Smart*. New York: Plume, 1999.

Arnheim, R. *Visual Thinking*. Berkeley, CA: University of California Press, 1969.

"Learning in the Arts" and "Student Academic and Social Development." 2002. Arts Education Partnership. www.aep-arts.org.

Barclay, K. D. "Constructing Meaning: An Integrated Approach to Teaching Reading." *Intervention in School and Clinic* 26.2 (1990): 84-91.

Beach, R., and J. Myers. *Inquiry-Based English Instruction: Engaging Student in Life and Literature*. New York: Teachers College Press, 2002.

Beers, K.. *When Kids Can't Read: What Teachers Can Do*. Portsmouth, NH: Heinemann, 2002.

Bell, N. *Visualizing and Verbalizing for Language Comprehension and Thinking*. San Luis Obispo, CA: Gander Educational Publishing, 1991.

Benton, M., and P. Benton. *Double Vision: Reading Paintings, Reading Poems, Reading Paintings*. London: Hodder and Stoughton, 1990.

Booth, W. *A Rhetoric of Irony*. Chicago: The University of Chicago Press, 1974.

Brown, J., A.. Collins, and P. Duguid. "Situated Cognition and the Culture of Learning." *Educational Researcher* 18 (1989): 32-42.

Bruner, J. *Actual Minds, Possible Worlds*. Cambridge, MA: Harvard University Press, 1986.

—. "From Communication to Language: A Psychological Perspective." *Cognition* 3 (1975): 255-287.

Collins, A., J. Brown, and S. Newman. "Cognitive Apprenticeship: Teaching the Crafts of Reading, Writing, and Mathematics." *Knowing, Learning and Instruction: Essays in Honor of Robert Glaser*. Ed. L. B. Resnick. Hillsdale, NJ: Lawrence Erlabaum, 1992. 453-94.

Fredericks, A. D. "Mental Imagery Activities to Improve Comprehension." *Reading Teacher* 40 (1986): 78-81.

Gambrell, L., and R. J. Bales. "Mental Imagery and the Comprehension Monitoring Performance of Fourth- and Fifth-Grade Poor Readers. *Reading Research Quarterly* XXI.4 (1986): 454-464.

Gambrell, L. B., and P. S. Koskinen. "Imagery: A Strategy for Enhancing Comprehension." *Comprehension Instruction: Research-Based Practices*. Eds. Block, C. C., and M. Pressley. New York: Guilford, 2002. 305-318.

Gardner, H. *Frames of mind: The Theory of Multiple Intelligences*. New York: Basic Books, 1983.

Geschwind, N. "Why Orton Was Right." *Annals of Dyslexia* 32 (1982): 13-30.

Hammond, J., and P. Gibbons. "What is Scaffolding?" *Scaffolding: Teaching and Learning in Language and Literacy Classrooms*. Ed. Hammond, J. Newton, AU: Primary English Teaching Association, 2001.

Hillocks, G. "Towards a Hierarchy of Skills in the Comprehension of Literature." *English Journal* 69 (1980): 54-59.

—. *Teaching Writing as Reflective Practice*. New York: Teachers College Press, 1995.

—. *The Testing Trap*. New York: Teachers College Press, 2001.

—. *Ways of Thinking/Ways of Teaching*. New York: Teachers College Press, 1999.

—. "The Writer's Knowledge: Theory, Research and Implications for Practice." *The Teaching of*

Writing: 85th Yearbook of the National Society for the Study of Education. Eds. Batholomae, D., and A. Petrosky. Chicago: University of Chicago Press, 1986. 71-94.

Hillocks, G., and M. W. Smith. "Sensible Sequencing: Developing Knowledge of Literature Text by Text." *English Journal* 77.6 (1988): 44-49.

Iser, W. *The Act of Reading: A Theory of Aesthetic Response.* Baltimore, MD: Johns Hopkins University Press, 1978.

Jerry, L., and A. Lutkus. The Nation's Report Card: Reading Highlights from the NAEPs, 2002: 2002 Reading Trends Differ by Grades. NCES 2003 524.

Kohn, A. *Beyond Discipline: From Compliance to Community.* Alexandria, VA: ASCD, 1996.

Lehrer, R. "Authors of Knowledge: Patterns of Hypermedia Design." *Computers as Cognitive Tools.* Eds., Derry, S., and S. Lajoie. Hillsdale, NJ: Lawrence Erlbaum, 1993. 197-227.

Long, S. A., P. N. Winograd, and C. A. Bridge. "The Effects of Reader and Text Characteristics on Reports of Imagery During and after Reading." *Reading Research Quarterly* 19 (1989): 353-372.

McCloud, S. *Understanding Comics: The Invisible Art.* New York: HarperCollins, 1994.

Mercer, N. *The Guided Construction of Knowledge: Talk Amongst Teachers and Learners.* Clevedon, UK: Multilingual Matters, 1995.

—. "Neo-Vygotskian Theory and Classroom Education." *Language, Literacy and Learning in Educational Practice.* Eds. Steirer, B., and J. Maybin. Clevedon, UK: Multilingual Matters, 1994.

Meek, M., et al. *Achieving Literacy: Longitudinal Studies of Adolescents Learning to Read.* London: Kegan Paul, 1983.

Meyer, M. *Changing Our Minds: Negotiating English and Literacy.* Urbana, IL: NCTE, 1996.

Ogle, D. "K-W-L Plus: A Strategy for Comprehension and Summarization." *Journal of Reading* 30 (1983): 626-631.

Rogoff, B., B. Matusov, and S. White. "Models of Teaching and Learning: Participation in a Community of Learners." *The Handbook of Cognition and Human Development.* Eds. Olson, D., and N. Torrance. Oxford UK: Blackwell, 1996. 388-414.

Rose, D. S., M. Parks, K. Androes, and S. D. McMahon. "Imagery-Based Learning: Improving Elementary Students' Reading Comprehension with Drama Techniques." *Journal of Educational Research* 94.1 (2000): 55.

Rosenblatt, L. *The Reader, The Text, The Poem.* Carbondale, IL: Southern Illinois University Press, 1978.

Sadoski, M. "The Natural Use of Imagery in Story Comprehension and Recall: Replication and Extension." *Reading Research Quarterly* 20.5 (1985): 658-667.

Smagorinsky, P. *Expressions: Multiple Intelligences in the English Class.* Urbana, IL: NCTE, 1991.

Smith, M. "Teaching the Interpretation of Irony in Poetry." *Research in the Teaching of English* 23.3: 254-272.

—. *Understanding Unreliable Narrators.* Urbana, IL: NCTE, 1991.

Smith, M. W. and Wilhelm, J.D. *Reading Don't Fix No Chevys: Literacy in the Lives of Young Men.* Portsmouth, NH: Heinemann, 2002.

Sulzby, E. "Children's Emergent Reading of Favorite Storybooks: A developmental Study." *Reading Research Quarterly* 20.4 (1985).

Tharp, R., and R. Gallimore. *Rousing Minds to Life.* New York: Cambridge University Press, 1988.

Tyler, R. *Basic Principles of Curriculum and Instruction.* Chicago: University of Chicago Press, 1949.

Van Lier, L. *Interaction in the Language Curriculum: Awareness, Autonomy and Authenticity.* London: Longman, 1996.

Vygotsky, L. *Mind in Society: The Development of Higher Psychological Processes*. Eds. Cole, M., V. John-Steiner, S. Scribner, and E. Souberman. Cambridge, UK: Cambridge University Press, 1978.

—. Trans. A. Kozulin. *Thought and Language*. Cambridge, MA: Harvard University Press, 1934/1986.

Wells, G. *Dialogic Inquiry: Toward a Sociocultural Practice and Theory of Education*. New York: Cambridge University Press, 1999.

Wiggins, G., and J. McTighe. *Understanding by Design*. Alexandria, VA: ASCD, 2001.

Whitin, P. *Sketching Stories, Stretching Minds*. Portsmouth, NH: Heinemann, 1996.

Wilhelm, J. *Action Strategies for Deepening Comprehension: Role Plays, Text-Structure Tableaux, Talking Statues, and Other Enactment Techniques That Engage Students With Text*. New York: Scholastic, 2002.

Wilhelm, J. *Improving Comprehension With Think Aloud Strategies: Modeling What Good Readers Do*. New York: Scholastic, 2001.

Wilhelm, J. *Inquiring Minds Want to Read and Write: Questioning, Talk and Classroom Inquiry That Improve Reading and Writing*. New York: Scholastic, forthcoming.

Wilhelm, J. "Reading IS Seeing." *Journal of Reading Behavior* 27.4 (1995): 467-503.

Wilhelm, J. *You Gotta BE the Book: Teaching Engaged and Reflective Reading with Adolescents*. New York: Teachers College Press, 1997.

Wilhelm, J., T. Baker, and J. Dube. *Strategic Reading: Guiding Students to Lifelong Literacy, Grades 6–12*. Portsmouth, NH: Heinemann, 2001.

Wilhelm, J. and B. Edmiston. *Imagining to Learn: Inquiry, Ethics and Integration Through Drama*. Portsmouth, NH: Heinemann, 1998.

Wilhelm, J. and P. Friedemann. *Hyperlearning: Where Projects, Inquiry and Technology Meet*. York, ME: Stenhouse, 1998.

Wood, D., J. Bruner, and G. Ross. "The Role of Tutoring in Problem-Solving." *Journal of Child Psychology and Psychiatry* 17 (1976).

Wright, B., D. Betteridge, and M. Buckby. *Games for Language Learning*. Cambridge, UK: Cambridge University Press, 1984.

LITERATURE CITED

Armstrong, Jennifer. 1998. *Shipwreck at the Bottom of the World: The Extraordinary True Story of Shackleton & the Endurance*. New York: Crown.

Bemelmans, Ludwig. 1939. *Madeline*. New York: Viking.

Bial, Raymond. 1995. *Underground Railroad*. New York: Houghton Mifflin.

Blumberg, Rhoda. 1998. *What's the Deal? Jefferson, Napoleon & the Louisiana Purchase*. National Geographic Society.

Blumberg, Rhoda. 1999. *Commodore Perry in the Land of the Shogun*. New York: HarperCollins Children's Books.

Bridges, Ruby. 1999. *Through My Eyes*. New York: Scholastic.

Bruchac, Joseph. 2002. *Navajo Long Walk: The Tragic Story of a Proud People's Forced March from Their Homeland*. National Geographic Society.

Burleigh, Robert. 2002. *Into the Air: The Story of the Wright Brother's First Flight*. New York: Harcourt Children's Books.

Clinton, Catherine. 1998. *I, Too, Sing America: Three Centuries of African American Poetry*. New York: Houghton Mifflin.

Colman, Penny. 2002. *Where the Action Was: Women War Correspondents in World War II*. New York: Crown.

Conrad, Pam. 1991. Prairie Visions: the Life and Times of Solomon Butcher. New York: Scholastic.

Corrigan, Paul. 1984. *At the Grave of the Unknown Riverdriver: Poems of the Upcountry*. North Country.

Cox, Clinton. *Fiery Vision: The Life and Death of John Brown*. (Out of Print)

Craddock, Jim. 2000. *Videohounds Golden Movie Retriever: The Complete Guide to Movies on Videocassette, DVD & Laserdisc*. Farmington Hills: Gale.

Curtis, Christopher Paul. 1999. *Bud, Not Buddy*. New York: Dell.

Fendler, Donn. 1992. *Lost on a Mountain in Maine*. New York: HarperCollins Children's Books.

Fendler, Donn. 1992. *Lost on a Mountain in Maine: A Brave Boy's True Story of His Nine-Day Adventure Alone in the Mountains*. New York: Turtleback.

Fleischman, Paul. 1995. *Bull Run*. New York: HarperCollins Children's Books.

Fleischman, Paul. 1996. *Dateline: Troy*. Boston: Candlewick.

Fleishman, John. 2002. *Phineas Gage: A Gruesome but True Story About Brain Science*. New York: Houghton Mifflin.

Florian, Douglas. 1999. *Laugh-Eteria: Poems & Paintings*. New York: Harcourt Children's Books.

Florian, Douglas. 2000. *Mammalabilia*. New York: Harcourt Children's Books.

Florian, Douglas. 1998. *Insectlopedia: Poems and Paintings*. New York: Harcourt Children's Books.

Ford, Richard. 1995. *Independence Day*. New York: Alfred A. Knopf.

Fradin, Dennis Brindell. 2000. *Bound for the North Star: True Stories of Fugitive Slaves*. New York: Houghton Mifflin.

Fradin, Dennis Brindell. 1997. *The Planet Hunters*. New York: Simon & Schuster.

Frank, E. R. 2002. *America*. New York: Atheneum Books for Children.

Freedman, Russell. 1994. *Kids at Work: Lewis Hine and the Crusade Against Child Labor*. New York: Houghton Mifflin.

George, Jean Craighead. 1991. *My Side of the Mountain*. New York: Penguin Putnam Books for Young Readers

Gerstein, Mordecai. 2002. *What Charlie Heard: The Story of the American Composer Charles Ives*. New York: Farrar, Straus & Giroux.

Gilliland, J. *Steamboat: The Story of Captain Blanch Leathers*. (Out of Print)

Golenbock, Peter. 1990. *Teammates*. New York: Lee & Low

Gollub, Matthew. 1998. *Cool Melons—Turn to Frogs! The Life & Poems of Issa*. New York: Lee & Low.

Greenberg, Jan and Sandra Jordan. 2002. *Action Jackson*. Millbrook: Millbrook Press.

Greenberg, Jan. 2003. *Romare Bearden: Collage of Memories*. New York: Harry N. Abrams.

Greenlaw, Linda. 1999. *The Hungry Ocean: A Swordboat Captain's Journey*. New York: Disney.

Greenlaw, Linda. 2002. *The Lobster Chronicles: Life on a Very Small Island*. Thorndike.

Hesse, Karen. 1999. *Out of the Dust*. New York: Scholastic.

Hinton, S. E. 1967. *The Outsiders*. New York: Viking.

Hinton, S. E. 1971. *That Was Then, This Is Now*. New York: Viking.

Hopkins, Lee Bennett. 2002. *Hoofbeats, Claws, & Rippled Fins*. New York: HarperCollins Children's Books.

Hoose, Phillip M. 2001. *We Were There, Too!*. New York: Dorling Kindersley.

Innocenti, Roberto and J. Patrick Lewis. 2002. *The Last Resort*. Mankato: Creative Editions.

Jakobsen, Kathy. 1998. *This Land Is Your Land*. New York: Little Brown.

Jenkins, Steve. 1998. *Hottest, Coldest, Highest, Deepest*. New York: Houghton Mifflin.

Jenkins, Steve. 2002. *The Top of the World: Climbing Mount Everest*. New York: Houghton Mifflin.

Junger, Sebastian. 1997. *The Perfect Storm: A True Story of Men Against the Sea*. New York: W. W. Norton.

Keats, Ezra Jack. 1990. *Peter's Chair*. New York: Penguin Putnam Books for Young Readers.

Kellog, Steven. 1992. *Mike Fink*. New York: HarperCollins Children's Books.

Koch, Kenneth and Kate Farrell. 1985. *Talking to the Sun: An Illustrated Anthology of Poems for Young People*. New York: Henry Holt Books for Young Readers.

Kennedy, X. J. and Dorothy M. Kennedy. 1999. *Knock at a Star: A Child's Introduction to Poetry*. New York: Little Brown.

Kurlansky, Mark. 1997. *Cod: A Biography of the Fish That Changed the World*. New York: Walker & Co.

Kurlansky, Mark. 1998. *Cod: A Biography of the Fish That Changed the World*. New York: Walker & Co.

Lasky, Kathryn. 2003. *A Voice of Her Own: The Story of Phyllis Wheatley, Slave Poet*. Boston: Candlewick.

Lear, Edward. 1871. *"The Owl and the Pussycat" in Nonsense Songs, Stories, Botany, and Alphabets*. London.

Lewis, C. S. 1959. *The Voyage of the Dawn Treader*. New York: MacMillan.

London, Jack. 1908. *"To Build a Fire" in The Youth's Companion*.

Lowry, Lois. 1990. *Number the Stars*. New York: Yearling Random House Children's Books.

McCullough, David. 2001. *John Adams*. New York: Simon & Schuster.

Medina, Tony. 2002. *Love to Langston*. New York: Lee & Low.

Mitchell, Margaree K. 1993. *Uncle Jed's Barber Shop*. New York: Simon & Schuster Books for Young Readers.

Moody, Anne. 1992. *Coming of Age in Mississippi*. New York: Dell.

Morrill, George. 1990. The Soldier Who Wouldn't Tell. In Read, 39(16), 22-31.

Murphy, Jim. 1993. *Across American on an Emigrant Train*. New York: Houghton Mifflin.

Murphy, Jim. 2000. *Blizzard! The Storm that Changed America*. New York: Scholastic.

Murphy, Jim. 1990. *The Boys' War: Confederate & Union Soldiers Talk about the Civil War*. New York: Houghton Mifflin.

Murphy, Jim. 1995. *The Great Fire*. New York: Scholastic.

Murphy, Jim. 1990. *The Long Road to Gettysburg*. New York: Houghton Mifflin.

Myers, Walter Dean. *At Her Majesty's Request: An African Princess in Victorian England*. New York: Scholastic.

Myers, Walter Dean. 1997. *Harlem: A Poem*. New York: Scholastic

Myers, Walter Dean. 1991. *Now Is Your Time! The African-American Struggle for Freedom*. New York: Turtleback.

O'Brien, Tim. 1990. *The Things They Carried*. New York: Houghton Mifflin.

Old, Wendie C. 2002. *To Fly: The Story of the Wright Brothers*. New York: Houghton Mifflin.

Parkman, Francis. 1982. *The Oregon Trail*. New York: Viking.

Partridge, Elizabeth. 1998. *Restless Spirit: The Life and Work of Dorothea Lange*. New York: Penguin Putnam Books for Young Readers.

Partridge, Elizabeth. 2003. *This Land Was Made for You and Me: The Life & Songs of Woody Guthrie*. New York: Viking Children's Books.

Peck, Richard. 2000. *A Year Down Yonder*. New York: Penguin Putnam Books for Young Readers.

Philip, Neil, ed. 2001. *Earth Always Endures: Native American Poems*.

Polacco, Patricia. 1994. *Pink and Say*. New York: Penguin Putnam Books for Young Readers.

Pringle, Laurence. 1995. Marcia Marshall, ed. *Dolphin Man: Exploring the World of Dolphins*. New York: Atheneum Books for Young Readers.

Rylant, Cynthia. 1994. *Something Permanent*. New York: Harcourt Children's Books.

Shaara, Michael. 1987. *Killer Angels*. New York: Ballantine.

Silverstein, Shel. 1974. "My Rules" in *Where the Sidewalk Ends*. New York: HarperCollins Children's Books.

Sneden, Robert Knox. Charles F. Bryan, Jr. & Nelson D. Lankford, eds. 2000. *Eye of the Storm: A Civil War Odyssey*. New York: The Free Press.

Stanley, Jerry. 1992. *Children of the Dust Bowl: The True Story of the School at Weedpatch Camp*. New York: Crown.

Stevens, Janet. 1995. *Tops and Bottoms*. New York: Harcourt Children's Books.

Stevens, Janet. 1996. *From Pictures to Words: A Book About Making a Book*. New York: Holiday House.

Taylor, Mildred. 1978. *Roll of Thunder, Hear My Cry*. New York: Viking.

Tillage, Leon W. 1997. *Leon's Story*. New York: Farrar, Straus & Giroux.

Turner, Ann Warren. 1997. *Dust for Dinner*. New York: Turtleback.

Van der Rol, Ruud and Rian Verhoeven. 1993. *Anne Frank, Beyond the Diary: A Photographic Remembrance*. New York: Penguin Putnam Books for Young Readers.

Wiesner, David. Dorothy Briley, ed. 1991. *Tuesday*. New York: Houghton Mifflin.

Wisniewski, David. 1991. *Sundiata: Lion King of Mali*. New York: Houghton Mifflin.

Wisniewski, David. *Sumo Mouse*. San Francisco: Chronicle.

White, E.B. 1974. *Stuart Little*. New York: HarperCollins Juvenile Books.

Wolfe, Tom. 2001. *The Right Stuff*. New York: Bantam.

X, Malcolm. 1964. *The Autobiography of Malcolm X, as Told to Alex Haley*. New York: Grove.

Index